# QUANTUM ESCHATON

GREGORY PETER LE SAGE

This is my first book. I want to thank ebookpbook for professional editing, good advice, and a high quality final product.

# Table Of Contents

# Chapter 1

# The Lab In The Woods

An austere-looking building dominates an open field, a stark contrast to the verdant forest surrounding it. Tall fences separate the compound from the primordial Siberian woods, patrolled by soldiers with machine guns slung over their backs. Military vehicles are parked in front of the building, and a huge Russian flag flutters above, a symbol of power and control. The serene green forest contrasts with the evil empire. The front of the building is marked by tall, black Cyrillic letters spelling out the words for "Kavka Laboratory."

лаборатория кавка

Inside the building, the lab is no less sterile. Fluorescent lights cast a harsh glare on polished floors. James Cathcart, thirty-three years old, is slim, though not especially fit. James is an engineer and looks the part. He wears a permanent scowl of worry. His shoulders are hunched, revealing his extreme fatigue.

James thinks carefully about what he is about to do. He considers alternatives and decides that he is about to take the only course of action that makes sense. This seems like a fitting end to a miserable existence. Despite all his efforts, James has never found love and acceptance. Only his work was successful. That was his only fulfillment. Now even that seems empty. No one will ever even know what he accomplished.

James looks at a workbench and exhales, closing his eyes for a moment. Alone in the laboratory, he shuts his laptop. He stands, reaching for a two- foot metal cylinder that controls the lab's overhead crane. His movements are precise and filled with a sense of urgency. James's face contorts and his shoulder twitches.

An eight-foot-high, four-foot-wide stainless steel dewar stands nearby, labeled жидкий гелий in Russian, which means "liquid helium." With the crane, James lifts the cylinder, breaking bolts on the ground with several loud pops. Tubes tear out of the vessel, and cryogenic liquid pours out, making crackling sounds as it hits the floor. The cryogenic liquid forms round puddles that race across the floor and evanesce. Swinging the cylinder across the room, James slams it into the only door of the laboratory with a resounding bang. He then drops the vessel on the ground with a crash and looks up at a security camera, flipping it off with a middle finger.

The dewar spews liquid helium, which crackles and fumes. The lab space is sealed, with a large vent above a workbench. James yanks the power cord to the vent fan from the wall, foiling any chance of survival. The spreading pool of liquid helium emits more gas.

# CHAPTER 2

# THE PURSUIT

In a nearby office is Natalia, a tall and lean thirty-year-old professional. She is conservatively dressed and wears a serious expression. Her desk is neat, and she has no pictures on any of the walls in her office. She is attractive but seems unaware of it. She is a no-nonsense professional. She picks up her phone and speaks excitedly in Russian. Monitors on her desk show men in green uniforms running down hallways in several directions. She bolts from her office, heading towards the source of the commotion.

Despite her commanding appearance, a storm brews within her— frustration mixed with an underlying concern for the man behind the sealed doors. James. Memories of past conversations and shared moments flicker in her mind.

Six men stand at a closed door in a hallway; one of them pushes against it. Natalia rounds the corner and barks, "Open this door!"

"We can't!" replies one of the soldiers.

"Do whatever you need to do but open it! Get a forklift or something," she commands.

The soldier raises his rifle to shoot the lock, but Natalia stops him. “No! No shooting. We need this man. We need him alive.” Cryogenic liquid leaks under the door into the hallway. Vapor rises at their feet. The soldiers step back in alarm.

“It won’t hurt us out here, but the sealed room is going to fill with helium quickly. He will be dead in minutes,” Natalia explains hurriedly. “You and you, find a forklift and drive it here. You, find an axe and bring it back.”

Natalia’s heart is pounding. She had grown to care about James. The way he looked at her made her know that he was thinking of her, too. She knew that their situation could never lead to a relationship, but she felt something for James that she had never felt before.

Natalia pounds the door with a fist and screams, “James!”

# CHAPTER 3

# A DESPERATE MOVE

Inside the lab, James climbs a platform and sits with his back against a frame, a calm smile spreading across his face. He breathes deeply on purpose, inhaling helium. James seems at peace with his fate.

With a smile, James says to himself, "Helium rises."

Memories flood his mind—Natalia's laughter, the warmth of shared moments, the dreams of a life never realized.

In the hallway, the Russian soldiers bang on the door and poke at the hinges. A man with a crowbar runs up. "Try to break the door. We only have a few minutes," Natalia orders.

She approaches the door and starts shouting in English, "James! This is Natalia. You don't have to do this. You don't have to die. We are going to let you go when this is over. You can have your life back."

James, sitting on the platform with his eyes closed, holds a small statue in his hand. A tear streams down his face. He shouts back, "Natalia, you know that's bullshit but thank you for saying it. We all know I am a dead man. You are the only person I trust, even love."

James imagines a different life where he is working with laboratory equipment next to Natalia. He dreams of having a family with smiling children. He dreams of love and acceptance. James grips the statue and stares at it. More tears. Instead, his life is about to end sadly.

James's voice changes due to the inhalation of helium, becoming higher pitched. He struggles to continue speaking. "This is the only way. I am sorry. до свидания," he says, which means "goodbye."

More wispy white cryogenic vapor escapes under the doors, and some of the soldiers in green uniforms step back.

# Chapter 4

## Six Months Earlier

The Alpheus Field Office in Seattle is modern but plain with no ornate distractions. The surroundings exude solemnity. It looks like a place where serious work gets done. Inside, people scurry around window-walled conference rooms, each with five to ten people sitting around huge flat screens, wearing identity badges. Large wooden double doors with multiple locks and illuminated warning signs indicate laboratory activity.

James, clean-shaven and well-rested, wears a nervous smile, trying to look comfortable in his surroundings. Charles Rogan, walking beside him, nods at passersby. Charles has a limp, which James notices, thinking of his own affliction. Charles has been an employee of Alpheus for several years and seems to know everyone. Charles is part of Alpheus Human Resources.

"This place is awesome. You have your own private Starbucks?" James asks, looking around wide-eyed.

"Yeah, it's kind of a scene. They want all your attention and all of your time. Food is free, too. Your special group is dedicated to passing data in and out of the qubits," Charles explains.

"I'm in a special group?" James asks.

"Separate from the rest of us. Seth Lawrence grabbed some really impressive people from national labs and universities. I mean, I think it's fair to say that you were stolen from Stanford. I'm sure they miss you," Charles replies.

"I doubt it," James says, glancing around.

"Seth is spending a lot of money to bring together some of the best minds," Charles continues as they walk past a glass-walled conference room with a gigantic flat screen on the wall. The face on it is much larger than life.

"I have never seen a screen that big," James comments. "They spare no expense here," Charles responds.

"Is Seth a scientist?" James inquires.

"No. Not exactly. I would call Seth a minister without a portfolio. He doesn't really have a specific job. He has made maneuvers for Alpheus that brought in a legendary amount of money. He's a pretty interesting guy. Kinda mysterious," Charles half whispers.

James thinks of what an enigmatic and awesome person Seth seems to be. The fact that Seth is directly involved in bringing him here means that Seth has just changed his life. Charles seems to be in awe of Seth. James has never known a person like this.

Inside an elevator, Charles places his ID card against a reader and presses a button separated from the regular floors. The elevator opens to a brightly lit white room with a single door, a camera staring down, and an eye scanner and keypad. Charles looks into the eye scanner, presses a button on the keypad, and the numbers scramble. He enters a 12-digit code, and with a loud click, large electric deadbolts operate in the door. The door then opens automatically.

Inside is a dimly lit room with multiple workbenches against the walls. Three people are working inside. "We will get you your own lab space, but you can get started right away. Seth will make sure you have the equipment and space that you want," Charles says.

James looks around, impressed. "What is this place? I have never seen such security."

"Like I said, your work is top priority. By the way, Seth is throwing a party this weekend. He told me to ask you to come. You can meet the other people on your team and some of us regular folks," Charles invites.

"He sounds pretty incredible," James remarks. "He is," Charles agrees, nodding.

# CHAPTER 5

# THE COMPANY PARTY

James stands alone next to a table with a drink in his hand. He looks visibly uncomfortable. Inside, he is even more uncomfortable. He wants to make a good impression on people, but honestly, he wishes he was alone and working. In this new life, he needs to try to be someone different. He needs to try to overcome his craving for solitude.

The table is covered with lavish food. Every neatly placed item is handcrafted. Grape leaf wraps, sushi, tiny bowls of poke. The palatial mansion exudes wealth. The lawns are absolutely perfect. Top-notch booze fills a hardwood table. A bottle of 1956 Armagnac sits prominently. Groups of three-four people gather at various locations, drinking and talking. Laughter drifts through the scene.

James can't shake the feeling of being an outsider in this place of wealth and power. Stanford was never like this. This is a new world.

Adira, a very beautiful woman, tall, dark-haired, athletic, and strong, spots James standing next to the food table. "Hey. You must be James. I am Adira," she greets cheerfully.

"Hi," James replies, forcing a smile even though he feels uncomfortable. "You're the guy from Stanford? Go trees!" she says.

"What?" James asks, confused. "Your mascot," Adira explains.

"Oh. I guess. I never really went to any games. I always thought it was a spear of asparagus." James grimaces and jerks his head.

Adira is surprised and a bit alarmed by James's physical display and asks, "Did something happen there?"

"Oh, I have a cramp in my arm from playing racquetball. It has been seizing up. Sorry. I'm OK," James lies.

"Oh, OK. Well, we're glad to have you, and I am glad to meet you," Adira says warmly.

"Thanks. So, what do you do?" James asks.

"A little bit of everything, but I work with Seth a lot. That's how I heard about you. I handle internal affairs for Alpheus. I am a problem solver," she replies.

"That sounds a bit scary," James remarks.

Just then, Seth walks by, exuding a vibe of a shark wearing Armani. "Speak of the devil. Let me introduce you," Adira says.

James marvels at Seth. He is so cool. This awesome place is his. Speak of the devil. Interesting choice of words.

James forces a grin. He is clearly not in his element. James and Adira walk up to Seth. Seth turns and smiles warmly at Adira. Adira turns and smiles coyly.

Seth is tall and handsome. He has thick, black hair and a carefully groomed beard. He looks fit and has broad shoulders. He stares intently at Adira as they stand close together.

"Seth, I want you to meet someone," says Adira. Seth puffs up his chest and grins widely.

"No introduction is necessary. James! I am so glad to see you here. I've been anxious to meet you," Seth greets warmly. Seth takes James's hand and tries to make him meet his gaze.

"Thanks. I have already heard a lot about you, too. It seems I owe you," James says.

"All you owe me is a brilliant invention. I'm going to make sure you have everything you need and want at Alpheus. Adira, can you please excuse us for a bit?" Seth asks.

"Of course. It was nice to meet you, James," Adira says.

James says, "Thank you, it was nice to…" but Adira walks away. James frowns and considers his usual inability to catch social queues.

Seth puts his arm around James and leads him to the bar. "Let me refresh your drink. You look a little nervous."

"Well, parties are not really my thing," James admits.

"Mine either. Bunch of phonies," Seth whispers, making James smile. "I read your papers and reviewed your career at Stanford. Extremely impressive. Our recruiters told me about your condition," he continues.

"Crap. I interview with people, and all they notice is Tourette syndrome?" James asks, frustrated.

"Well, people notice. If they are not used to it, it gets their attention. Just let me say up front that I consider it irrelevant. At Alpheus, you are a respected scientist. That's all that matters," Seth assures him.

"I'm glad you brought it out in the open. Maybe sometime I can do a Tourette show. I bet it would be good for a laugh," James jokes.

Seth pours a drink for James, a complicated mixture of four kinds of alcohol. He skewers a piece of pineapple with a tiny umbrella and puts it in the glass. He hands it to James.

"People know you are with me. Nobody is ever going to fuck with you. You are one of my special people," Seth explains. "I wanted to meet you and assure you that all that counts here is your ability. You are welcome here, you are respected, and I will make sure that people do what you want."

"That is very reassuring. I feel a little bit overwhelmed, but I can see that I am starting a new, better life," James says.

"I have a couple of people I need to talk to. Do you see Charles over there? Ask him to introduce you to some of the people in your new group," Seth instructs.

"Thanks, Seth," James says, and Seth quickly turns and walks away.

Seth is everything James expected. The world bows down to this guy. He saw Adira's expression when she met Seth earlier. She is obviously into him. James can't believe he is giving him attention.

James approaches Charles with his fancy new drink. "Hi, Charles. What's happening?" James greets.

"Just digging the scene. Let me introduce you to some of your teammates. Do you see that woman over there? Her name is Parvati. She is a programming wizard. We stole her from Oracle. She used to program algorithms for high-speed stock market trades. Before that, she was famous for her PhD work in artificial intelligence," Charles explains as they walk up to Parvati.

"Parvati, hello. It's nice to see you this evening," Charles greets. "Hello, Charles. Who is this with you?" Parvati asks.

"This is James, the new guy from Stanford," Charles introduces.

"Hello, James. I read a few of your papers. I'm glad you are on our team," Parvati says enthusiastically.

Parvati's eyes glint with intelligence and a hint of mischief. James thinks he should be careful. Parvati is slender and attractive. James imagines that a lot of men must pay attention to her at work.

"Hi. Thanks. I heard you came from Oracle. I bet that was fun," James replies.

"Oracle was OK, but working here is a lot more fun and interesting. We have a single, serious goal. This is our Manhattan project. They put a bunch of smart people in the wilderness, and they are hoping we can make the bomb," Parvati says.

"Well, I haven't really thought of it that way, but I can see an analogy. Are you going for assembly or implosion?" James asks.

"Definitely implosion. We are stuck with the most complicated thing there is. Like the bomb, it all has to work perfectly and synchronize. We want to talk to you about communication with qubits," Parvati explains.

"If this team is as dedicated as the scientist at Los Alamos, this is really going to be something," James remarks.

"That is how it is. We are a team, and now we are glad to have you, too," Parvati says.

"Thanks, Parvati. You are quite the effective advertisement for the group.

That was awesome," Charles says. "I try," Parvati says, smiling.

As they stand talking to Parvati, another man approaches. Noam, a very young man with a serious expression, slightly overweight with dark circles under his eyes, joins them.

"Oh, James, this is Noam. He just finished school. His PhD was on developing a machine learning algorithm that solved signal processing of computer communication in highly noisy environments. Noam does signal processing for our qubit communication," Charles introduces.

"Hello, James. I have heard a lot about you. It's nice to meet you," Noam greets.

"Thank you. I feel like everybody knows me, but I don't know anybody," James replies.

"OK guys, I'm off. See you around," Parvati says, nodding and walking away. Charles also nods and leaves. James and Noam face each other.

"Probably like you, I manage to be a little out of place and uncomfortable around here. You will find that at Alpheus, it is not looked down upon. Thank goodness for that. I know some people, but I pretty much do my own thing," Noam says.

"Well, that sounds familiar. I'm glad it's OK," James says.

"This place has its perks. I saw you talking to Adira. How did you pull that off? She is so hot," Noam asks.

"She introduced herself to me. I think Seth put her up to it," James explains.

"If I were you, I would have attached myself to her all night," Noam says. "Well, that wasn't really in the cards. Aren't there other girls around?"

James asks.

"Are you kidding me? The chance of me meeting a girl here is about as good as our group making a quantum computer that cracks encryption," Noam replies.

"You don't think we are going to succeed?" James asks, surprised.

"This is an extremely hard problem. You can buy all the smart people in the world, but it doesn't create magic sauce," Noam says.

"I know a lot about it. It's good to hear some honesty," James says, appreciating Noam's frankness.

"Well, I'm going to leave you to it," Noam says.

"It was good to meet you. I will see you around," James replies.

James feels a sense of belonging, a glimmer of hope that perhaps he has found his place among these brilliant misfits. He also has a head full of ideas about quantum computing. He can tell that he knows some things that these people don't.

Being alone for a moment, James sees his opportunity to slip away. He smiles and sips his drink as he walks across the courtyard. He finds an open sliding glass door. He places his glass on a table and makes his way to an exit.

# CHAPTER 6

# NEW BEGINNINGS

James walks through the bustling Alpheus field office in Seattle, the ID badge on his chest bumping with each step. As he reaches the door to his new lab, a man approaches him in the hallway.

"James, I'm Ethan," the man says. "I'm the hardware guy for your group.

I take care of cryogenics and electronics."

James extends a hand, but Ethan just looks at him. James lowers his hand and offers a polite smile. "Well, it's good to meet you. I'm just starting a new lab."

Ethan's expression hardens. "I noticed you talked a lot to Seth. Did he tell you that you can push us around? I want you to know that I can't be pushed around."

James raises his hands in a calming gesture. "I'm not going to push anybody anywhere. I just want to work with people and get things done."

Ethan nods, but his eyes remain wary. "Well, you should know that I have my own job. I do it well, and I don't want anyone telling me what to do."

"Ethan, we just met. I'm not here to cause trouble for you. I want to work with you so that we both succeed," James assures him.

"Well, as long as we understand each other," Ethan replies before spinning on his heel and walking away.

James notices Parvati standing nearby, observing the interaction. She approaches him with a sympathetic smile.

"Don't worry. He does that to everybody," she says reassuringly.

James just really hopes that Alpheus will be something new, not the hard times he is accustomed to. A bent-out-of-shape tech is not so bad. The guy basically has to do what James tells him, so this should not be a problem. It's more acceptance from his peers that James hopes for.

# CHAPTER 7

# SURVEILLANCE AND TRUST

An Alpheus seCurity room is dimly lit, filled with the soft glow of numerous monitors displaying various angles of the field office. Seth and Adira watch the screens intently. One monitor shows a time-lapse of James working in his lab, the 24-hour clock on the wall marking late-night hours. Equipment gradually fills the lab in time-lapse, evidence of James's relentless work ethic.

"I reviewed some footage. James works at night all the time," Adira comments, her eyes never leaving the screen.

"I didn't hire him for nine to five," Seth responds, a hint of admiration in his voice.

Adira's gaze shifts to another monitor. "I also notice that he is not interacting much with anyone else."

Seth shrugs. "I'm not sure he needs anybody else. I have a lot of confidence in James. I talked to Ethan about what he's been installing. James has been setting up a microwave probe system tied to a dilution refrigerator. He's manipulating qubits. He hasn't been asking anyone for help."

Adira raises an eyebrow. "James already knows that you have free run of this place. He won't be surprised if you just pop in to talk to him."

"I don't want to invade his space," Seth says, almost to himself. Adira chuckles softly. "Seth, we are spying on him."

Seth sighs, acknowledging the irony. "Yes. And see how happy he is?

What did you two talk about at my party?"

As they monitor James's activities, Seth's mind races. He sees potential in James, a spark that others overlook. His conversation with Adira is laced with subtle tension, an undercurrent of shared secrets and unspoken agendas. For Seth, the stakes are high, and every decision carries weight. As they watch James at work, Seth feels a surge of confidence in the path he has chosen.

"I tried to joke around with him a little. I told him you do whatever you want," Adira admits.

"Oh, I'm sure that put him at ease," Seth replies with a smirk.

Adira leans closer, her eyes serious. "Well, Seth, it's pretty much true.

He needs to know a little about who you are."

Seth meets her gaze, their proximity charged with unspoken tension. "And who do you think I am?"

The moment lingers. Adira stares at Seth, a flirtatious grin creeping across her lips.

Seth steps closer. He considers caressing her but knows he must control himself. Adira is clearly thinking the same thing. Seth returns her grin and nods. He finally breaks the silence. "OK. I will talk to James. Maybe he will let me into his lab."

They are both relieved that the moment of physical tension has passed. Adira nods approvingly. "That would be a good idea."

Seth and Adira have clearly agreed to keep things professional. Their familiarity shows that there has been a lot more between them previously.

# CHAPTER 8

# THE QUANTUM FRONTIER

In an expansive conference room of Alpheus Headquarters, a long, dark hardwood table is surrounded by plush, high-back chairs. About fifteen people sit along the table's edges, their attention focused on a man standing by a wall covered with a huge flat monitor displaying several graphs. Seth sits near the front. The plush conference room contrasts with the more plain field office. Phillip, a man who has seen better days, stands at the front. His clothes are high class, but a pot belly and thinning hair reveal the passage of time.

"Gentlemen, you are all familiar with the importance of quantum computing. Alpheus is all in on this. We intend to be the winners. I brought you here today to learn about your progress. I need you to explain where we are and what needs to happen," Phillip declares, his tone commanding.

Seth leans forward. "Phillip, as you know, I have been bringing in the best minds around to make this work. I have some really exciting new hires, and I am confident that we will make progress."

Phillip nods, but his eyes are skeptical. "I know you are spending a lot of money."

"My spending is very strategic. A new guy named James was already making progress in his last job at Stanford. They were not smart enough to pay attention. He has some new concepts about interacting with qubits in non-destructive ways. That's the one thing that has stopped everyone else so far," Seth explains.

Phillip's expression softens slightly. "I'm glad to hear that, but I want to know when we will cross the finish line."

"This is the most cutting-edge research. I can't set a date for success. Big discoveries happen suddenly. Everything could change tomorrow," Seth responds, his voice steady.

Another man, Alfred, shuffles papers on the table, clearly wanting to speak. He wears thick prescription glasses with heavy black frames. Alfred is clearly on the technical side of this effort. "Google and IBM have both made noise recently about what they say is important progress in quantum computing. They make it sound like they are already close to success."

"That's all bush-league bullshit. Their best machines are a few qubits. They are millions of times too small to do anything important. If you double nothing, it's still nothing. We need a robust qubit system that is stable and can be expanded significantly," Seth counters, his tone sharp.

Phillip nods thoughtfully. "That's fine. Our machine needs to be better.

Just know that this is not a science project. We want R.O.I."

Seth considers how to keep management at bay. He has his own plans. "Just keep giving me money and stay out of my way," Seth thinks. Seth comes back to the present, looks around, smiles, and exclaims, "We have the best team and the best plans. Your return on investment is going to shock you and the whole world."

# CHAPTER 9

# EXECUTIVE CONFRONTATION

James enters the office of Christopher, an executive at Alpheus, with whom he has an appointment. He is nervous talking to such an important person. Taking a deep breath, he exhales slowly, trying to relax. Christopher welcomes him in and directs an upturned palm to a chair in front of his desk.

James sits.

"I want to present my new work on qubit communication. I have made some progress. I know there is a big meeting next week," James says to Christopher.

"James, we are excited about your progress. Maybe you can ask someone on your team to present the results," Christopher replies.

"Wait. This is my work. Why don't I present it?" James asks, confusion creeping into his voice.

"Maybe you can give a more junior person on your team a chance," Christopher suggests.

"With all due respect, sir, this is my work, and I should present it," James says, scowling.

"James, this is a really big presentation with a lot of people." Christopher frowns.

"What is this about? Do you not want people to see me?" James asks, frustration building.

"James, this is uncomfortable, and I'm sorry, but a lot of people don't know about your condition, and they are going to be uncomfortable," Christopher replies, his forehead wrinkling.

"Seth told me Tourette was not a problem and that I would be respected here. This is upsetting," James says. He leans forward and stares at Christopher just as his face twitches.

"James, you are respected. Everyone thinks you are great. I just need this presentation to get the kind of attention we need," Christopher replies. "If it were up to me, this wouldn't be a problem. But—if I can be honest and go off the record—these investors are like sharks; they sniff out any sort of weakness. Legally, I can't ask you not to present, but…"

"Well, asking some junior person to present my work is wrong. I don't want to do that." James tightens a fist.

"Please talk it over with Seth then. The board was pretty clear with me about this," Christopher replies.

"So, the whole board wants to keep me in hiding. That's great. Excuse me, sir, but I need to leave." James stands up stiffly.

"I'll let Seth figure this out then. Please understand that I and we all have great respect for you," Christopher offers.

"I will talk to Seth. Thank you," James says as he walks out.

James texts Seth and asks for an urgent meeting. The symbol for Seth on James's phone is an exclamation mark. Seth replies quickly and affirmatively. They meet at an Alpheus coffee shop.

"Seth, Christopher told me that he wants my work presented, but not by me," James says, frustration evident in his voice.

"Yeah, I heard about it. It's not going to happen, James. I have a plan," Seth replies, a reassuring smile on his face.

"I want you to present. I am going to set things up in a special way. I have arranged the use of our largest auditorium at headquarters. It has a tall stage. The audience is below the speaker. The distance from the speaker to the first row is about 20 feet. The screen is huge. I am going to make the room dark and the screen bright. You are going to present your own work. If you're having a problem, turn towards the screen until you regain composure. Just keep talking. Don't let anyone see what's happening to you."

"Seth, that sounds like a good idea. If I can hide my Tourette, everything will be fine. Can you convince the board to let this happen?" James asks, hope flickering in his eyes.

"To some extent, they just listen to me. If I say this should happen, they will go along with it," Seth replies confidently.

The bond between them strengthens in that moment. James feels a deep sense of gratitude and loyalty towards Seth. His power is also impressive, as always. Alpheus is a major corporation, and Seth just tells people what to do.

# CHAPTER 10

# THE PRESENTATION

The day of the presentation arrives. James stands behind the curtain, taking deep breaths to calm his nerves. The auditorium is packed, the dim lights and large screen creating an almost cinematic atmosphere. Seth has kept his promise. The setup is perfect.

"Good luck," Seth whispers, giving James a reassuring pat on the back before stepping away.

James walks onto the stage, the bright lights obscuring his view of the audience. He begins his presentation, his voice steady despite the pressure. As he speaks, he feels the familiar twinge in his muscles—the urge to tic. Following Seth's advice, he turns towards the screen, allowing the audience to focus on his slides. Thankfully, James's version of Tourette doesn't include speech problems. He sounds perfectly normal. He points his twitching shoulder towards the bright screen so no one notices.

He continues, smoothly transitioning through each point. The room is silent, the audience fully engaged. James feels a surge of confidence. The occasional tics were there, but he managed to hide them, maintaining his composure.

As he reaches the conclusion, summarizing the key points and potential impact of the project, a sense of relief washes over him. The final slide displays a concise summary, and he takes a deep breath.

"Thank you for your time. I'm happy to answer any questions," James concludes, stepping back and letting the room absorb the information.

The applause that follows is heartfelt, and James feels a wave of pride. Despite the challenges, he has done it. The first question comes. James pulls up a slide and turns towards the screen as he speaks, hiding a facial twitch.

More questions come, each one allowing him to showcase his knowledge and commitment. The room buzzes with excitement and approval.

After the last question, James gathers his notes, a sense of accomplishment settling over him. He faced his fears and his condition, and he succeeded. As he leaves the auditorium, several colleagues approach, offering congratulations and words of encouragement.

"Great job, James. You handled that beautifully," says Parvati, patting James's shoulder.

"Thanks, Parvati," he replies, his smile genuine. "It means a lot."

He steps out into the hallway, the weight of the presentation lifting. James feels like he at least set one thing straight in his otherwise mean and sad existence. He is grateful to Seth, who made this happen.

# CHAPTER 11

# CONFRONTATION WITH ETHAN

James walks down a brightly lit hallway at Alpheus, the echo of his footsteps the only sound in the otherwise silent corridor. Suddenly, Ethan, the hardware specialist who had previously harassed him, steps into his path, blocking his way.

"James, I was told to work this weekend on your new dewar. I missed something important," Ethan says, his voice laced with frustration.

"I wasn't told about that. I'm sorry," James replies, his tone apologetic yet cautious.

Ethan's eyes narrow, and he takes a step closer to James. "I told you before that I will not be pushed around. You are not so damn important that I should have to work on a weekend."

James instinctively takes a step back, feeling the tension rise. Just then, he notices Seth approaching from behind Ethan, his presence giving silent but powerful support.

"You are one of these special people that Seth thinks can make everybody do what they want. Well, I'm not going to play that game. You depend on me for your shit to work. You should back off,"

Ethan continues, his anger boiling over as he jabs James in the chest with his forefinger.

"Excuse me." Seth's calm voice cuts through the hostility. Ethan spins around, his face draining of color as he faces Seth.

"How would you like to get fired today?" Seth asks, his tone serene yet undeniably authoritative. He stands motionless, an unyielding figure of power.

Ethan's bravado evaporates instantly. "I'm sorry. I was just upset. It was a bad display. I'll get the work done," he stammers, his eyes lowered in submission.

"See that you do," Seth replies firmly. Ethan turns and walks away, his shoulders slumped.

James lets out a breath he hadn't realized he was holding. "Seth, thank you so much for defending me," he says.

Seth nods, his stern expression softening slightly. "You don't need to thank me, James. We're a team, and we look out for each other. Just remember to stand your ground next time. Bullies like Ethan feed off fear. I will always back you up."

James nods, taking in Seth's words. The encounter has shaken him.

# Chapter 12

# In Confidence

Seth is surprised to find James just outside his office door. James is, coincidentally, about to knock as Seth is leaving.

"Seth, I need to talk to you. Can we go into your office?" says James. "Sure. I was going to go talk to some guys. I don't have a schedule," Seth replies.

James and Seth walk into the office, and Seth closes the door. James looks around.

"This is going to be very private. Are we safe talking here?" asks James. "I have my office checked for bugs every once in a while. This should be a pretty safe place," Seth responds as he sits behind his desk.

"Good. Seth, you have been very good to me, and I trust you. I'm having a problem. Maybe a crisis. I feel like I'm not cutting the mustard," James says with a serious expression.

"James, you are doing great. What's this all about?" asks Seth.

"The talk went well, but maybe all those people who won't listen to me and don't want me to talk are right. Maybe nobody wants me around. I need to get a clue," says James with a sad expression.

He continues, "I was an only child. I was adopted. I don't know where my smarts come from. My parents might have adopted me just for the benefits. I didn't feel loved. I devoted myself to my work. I have never had a girlfriend and never made close friends."

"James, my friend, I have seen the people who give you a hard time. I want to punch each one of them in the balls. You are a brilliant scientist with a bright future. You are also a great person, and I like you a lot and think very highly of you. You are on the cusp of eternal greatness. I am doing my best to grease the skids to get you there. I, for one, have full confidence in you. I want to hear everything you have to say. You have seen how people treat me. They are both impressed and afraid. I am highly respected. This highly respected person is telling you that you are great and you are worth everything it takes to help. When you feel low, think of me. I am a big fan." Seth smiles and leans back in his chair.

"You know, Seth, you have been better to me than anyone ever has, including my parents," James says sadly.

"James, you're not young enough to be my kid, but I do hope to be like a father to you. All you need in life is respect and a little help," Seth replies.

"Seth, you are the most important person in my life. I will follow you anywhere," James says, looking like he is about to cry.

"James, that is a wonderful compliment. You should find strength in our friendship. Anyone who is in your way is noise. We are signal. Remember that," Seth replies.

Seth thinks to himself that James is just the person he has been looking for. James is going to do something great, and Seth is going to make the most of it. He feels a little guilty for so consciously arranging this situation with a Tourette sufferer, but like everything else in his life, he has a goal and a plan.

# Chapter 13

# Breakthrough

James works alone for months. Seth's promise of providing everything he needs has been truly fulfilled. James has never had such complete and modern apparatus. He is free to try new ideas, and there are no distractions. He continues the work he started at the SLAC National Accelerator Laboratory. James eats dinner at Alpheus and works most nights. There is a gym he never uses, but it has a locker room with showers. James keeps several sets of clothes in a big locker. Work is his life.

Most importantly, James has explored swept terahertz probing of quantum states. He was working on this at SLAC before he left. No one cared. Now it matters. He can successfully interrogate a state without destroying it. That is the real key to success. He has also transitioned to using lattice vacancies to make qubits. That has allowed him to radically increase the number of qubits that he uses. His apparatus is now small considering the number of qubits. He is exceeding everything he reads about other companies. James knows what he is doing is special. This inspires him to keep working.

In his lab, James is engrossed in his work, watching the oscilloscope trace intently. He turns knobs and presses buttons, adjusting the equipment with precision. Suddenly, a sharp peak appears on the oscilloscope trace. James's face breaks into a broad smile, and he pounds the table with his fist in triumph.

"YES!" he exclaims, unable to contain his excitement.

James double-checks his setup, disconnecting and reconnecting cables, adjusting knobs back and forth. His smile grows even bigger as he confirms his results. Rocking back in his chair, he lets out a deep breath, feeling the surge of his achievement.

The memory of his time at SLAC floods back. James rocks back in his chair and dreams about his former life.

# CHAPTER 14

# FLASHBACK

In a well-lit laboratory room at SLAC, workbenches line every wall, and a computer desk sits in the middle. James is motioning towards his work on the desk, clearly enthusiastic. His colleague, Thomas, stands over his shoulder, listening.

"Thomas, I'm getting closer to being able to manipulate and maintain qubits. That's the thing no one has been able to figure out," James says, his hands waving expressively.

Thomas nods, glancing at the computer screen. "Well, I'm a microwave guy, so I don't understand this in detail. You're in this lab day and night. I hope you are making progress."

"I am. It's really exciting. I have had this idea about using microwaves in a whole new way," James explains.

"I'm glad microwaves have something to do with it. Is anyone working on this with you?" Thomas asks.

"No. I'm OK working alone. So, the thing about a qubit is that it has to be able to maintain a superposition state that is very carefully affected by a quantum algorithm. Any external influence can make the state collapse. Measurement makes it collapse," James says, pointing to a poster on the wall.

"I do understand what qubits are. I have read that they are difficult to maintain. How are microwaves helping you?" Thomas inquires.

"A quantum non-demolition measurement or QND couples an observable property to another quantum system such as an electromagnetic field. My first trick was to discover what minimal microwave power level could measure anything about a quantum state without destroying it. My next innovation was quickly sweeping microwave frequency in the terahertz region," James explains, pointing to an oscilloscope trace on a workbench next to a large stainless-steel cylinder bolted to the floor.

"I work with terahertz. We mostly spend our time trying to make more power. I'm more of a source guy than an application guy," Thomas says.

"Terahertz sources are hard to make and produce very little power, but it's plenty for this job. The frequency agility that I required forced me to develop my own sources. By sweeping the frequency, I noted resonant behavior. The qubit reacts slightly differently over a wide range of frequencies. Those differences tell you about the state," James elaborates.

Thomas nods, but James's face winces noticeably, and his head jerks.

Standing very close, this display startles Thomas. He takes a step back.

"I'm sorry. That happens when I get excited. It's not painful. It just looks weird," James apologizes.

"Someone told me you had a twitch. I had just never seen it. You can't make it stop?" Thomas asks.

"It's called Tourette syndrome. No, I can't stop it at all," James explains. "OK. Go ahead and continue," Thomas offers, not sounding particularly interested.

James's enthusiasm dims as he realizes Thomas isn't fully engaged. "So, anyway, I am making progress reading quantum states without destroying them. I am using swept terahertz signal sources. It's new. No one else is doing this."

Thomas takes a step away from James and looks over his shoulder at the door. James notices and stops talking for a moment.

"It's not like I'm going to hurt you. It's just a twitch," James implores. "I don't care about the twitch. It's OK," Thomas replies.

James knows this isn't true. Once again, his work is ignored because he has a physical problem. This has happened so many times in his life, and he is really sick of it.

Thomas looks over his shoulder at the door again. James's shoulders droop as he realizes that Thomas has really stopped listening. James continues speaking but in a deflated, defeated way.

"So, anyway, I am making progress reading quantum states

without destroying them. I am using swept terahertz signal sources. It's new. No one else is doing this," James says.

"I appreciate you sharing this with me. I hope you are successful," Thomas replies, looking at his watch.

"Thanks. Well, I know you're a busy guy. I'm sure you need to go. Thanks for stopping by." James's shoulders droop again.

Thomas nods and turns away. As the door closes, James holds his head in his hands, feeling the sting of dismissal. This same scene has played out so many times for James.

# CHAPTER 15

# REALITY CHECK

James snaps baCk to reality, taking a deep breath. His sad memory is at least now only a memory. Maybe things will change now. He looks back at his oscilloscope, and a smile returns to his face. He decides to take a break and heads out to buy a cup of coffee, carefully locking his lab door. In the hallway, he encounters Noam.

"James! How's it going? Are you making progress?" Noam asks cheerfully.

"Well, a little. It's slow going," James lies.

"I need to know more about your qubit probing technique. I can help you decipher the outputs," Noam offers.

"I will be sure to tell you what I find. I'm getting closer," James says, very conscious of his deception.

"I look forward to hearing about it," Noam says as he walks away.

James watches him go, feeling a pang of guilt. He unlocks his lab door and steps back inside, his mind racing.

Seth has been clear about being secretive. James doesn't

understand why, but Seth gets what Seth wants. James owes him big time. In his mind, Seth comes before anything else.

James takes out his mobile phone and presses a button to call Seth. "Seth, this is James. I want you to come down to my lab," he says. "Sure. What's up?" Seth replies.

"You wanted me to speak carefully. I'd rather talk to you in person," James says.

"Understood. That's a good idea. I will be right down," Seth agrees.

James waits excitedly, his shoulder twitching. He grabs his arm with his other hand, trying to suppress the Tourette symptoms. He breathes deeply to relax. The lab door makes a loud CLICK as the electric locks open and Seth walks in. James is seated next to a tall stainless-steel cylinder connected by insulated tubes.

# CHAPTER 16

# THE BIG REVEAL

"Seth, thanks for coming. This is going to take a little while, so make yourself comfortable. What you care about is that I have broken RSA encryption," James says.

Seth's eyes widen in surprise. "That's years away. Some say decades." "Well, I did it. I can show you," James replies confidently.

Seth pulls up a chair next to James.

"Quantum computers are all about superposition, amplitudes, quantum entanglement, and quantum interference. Have you heard of Schrödinger's cat?" James begins.

"Of course. Everyone knows that story. The cat is both dead and alive, and its state is determined when you open the box," Seth responds.

"It is a good illustration of quantum states. That is the big difference between this and regular computers. Qubits can have multiple, simultaneous values, unlike bits. That's what makes quantum computers exponentially more powerful. Google and IBM have made quantum computers with just a few qubits. I have millions," James explains, resting his hands on the computer.

"On top of all the engineering, I needed to understand how to program a quantum computer. That is a matter of making sure that for every wrong answer, some of the paths leading to that answer have positive amplitudes and others have negative amplitudes so that, on the whole, they cancel each other out. All paths leading to the correct answer should reinforce each other with amplitudes pointing in the same direction. Once the algorithm finishes, you observe the states, which collapses them to single values," James continues, pointing at his oscilloscope showing a tall peak against low-level noise.

"Accelerated computing enabled emulation of quantum computers, so I could test algorithms that I created. The emulators are, of course, nowhere near as fast as a real quantum computer, but you can test individual steps. A design needs a simulator. An algorithm needs an emulator. These systems let you imagine what you can do once a real system is made," James explains.

"This peak represents a good answer to an algorithm. This computer screen shows the arrangement of the qubits," he continues, pointing to a large computer screen displaying graphics representing qubits linked with lines that symbolize quantum entanglement. Pulses of light race around the screen, representing the execution of the algorithm. Above the qubit diagram is a computer logic flow chart. A graphic shows steps proceeding in the program as the qubits interact.

"The thing about programming is that it is completely separate from making a computer work. A programmer doesn't need to know how to design a transistor. He doesn't even need to know about electricity. His job is logic. Quantum computers were proposed by Richard Feynman in the 1980s. He proposed the idea that a quantum computer would be the only way to simulate impossibly complicated physical systems. Neil Gershenfeld from MIT was part of making the first two-bit quantum computer in 1998. It could be loaded with data and output a solution. I have known what a quantum computer is for my whole life. I have thought about programming one as long as I can remember," James expounds passionately.

Seth watches with interest, though he looks slightly confused. James smiles, understanding the complexity.

"I know it's complicated. The point is, it's working. I figured out how to make millions of stable qubits that I can interact with. So, let me tell you about RSA public key encryption."

"I know all about RSA. It is the standard of encryption. Two big, secret, prime numbers. Multiply them together to make a public key. You use my public key to encrypt a message. Only I can decrypt the message with one of the prime factors that I have stored. I use your public key to send a message to you," Seth interrupts.

"Right. If a new computer can factor my public key, my message encryption is broken," James continues, pointing to a whiteboard with graphs. A cartoon compares traditional and quantum computers.

"A prime number 313 digits long takes sixteen million years to factor. If supercomputers get 10,000 times faster, so what? Even a few years might as well be forever. A traditional computer makes one computation at a time. A quantum computer considers all the possible answers at the same time. A system with N qubits considers 2 to the N possibilities. A 63-qubit computer is equivalent to almost 10 to 19 bits. A 3 GHz computer would take ninety- eight years to go through those bits," James explains, pacing back and forth.

"The numbers are great, but you know the only thing anyone cares about is what you can do with it. What is this giant thing?" Seth asks, standing up next to the tall cylindrical dewar. "Is Walt Disney frozen in here?"

"This machine is a dilution refrigerator. It keeps the quantum computer at 2 milli Kelvin," James explains.

"Why do you need that?" Seth asks, looking puzzled. James pauses, realizing that he is losing Seth's attention.

"That's as close to absolute zero as anyone ever gets. The trick is to keep the qubits isolated from the world outside. I built a much smaller one that is also working," James says.

"How small?" Seth asks.

"It should fit in the trunk of your car," James replies.

"Most researchers estimated that stable, reliable quantum computing would take one to two decades to work. I have it working today. I can break RSA," James adds.

Seth hands James a thumb drive. "Here's some encrypted data. Show me."

James uploads Seth's data. The computer screen shows the calculation proceeding, data streaming, with paths highlighting and darkening. James turns to Seth.

"The quick brown fox jumped over the lazy dog," James announces. "Damn. You got it. That was 256 bits! What did that take? Ten seconds?"

Seth says in amazement.

"You didn't just happen to have a thumb drive with a single encrypted message on it," James notes.

"No. I was expecting this. I'm surprised but not surprised," Seth admits. "You actually thought I was going to figure this out?" James asks.

"This is why I hired you. I expected great things," Seth replies. "You have a few other messages on there. Shall I break more?" "Please!" Seth urges.

James uploads another message. The computer graphics show data flowing between qubits and the path converging with illuminated lines. Both men watch the graphics.

"Three can keep a secret if two of them are dead," James reads. "You got it!" Seth exclaims. "That one's a little grim."

"Benjamin Franklin. What a kidder," James quips, repeating the process.

The computer graphics show the development of the solution path. "I love the smell of napalm in the morning," James announces. "I love Robert Duvall. You got it again," Seth responds.

Seth looks at James with admiration. "James, I know you face a lot of difficulties in your life due to Tourette syndrome. I have said it before, but to me, that problem is totally irrelevant. I want you to know that I really value you as an engineer and as a person. I am so glad I found you. You belong with me. Not only are you an engineering genius, but you are a programming genius. Anyone who has ever stood in your way is a fucking fool. They should have kissed your feet and kissed your ass, and they should have thrown rose petals everywhere you fucking walked. You deserve to have every single thing in life that you want right now."

"Wow. Those are some serious compliments. I haven't noticed any rose petals in my life so far," James says, amused.

"I need to talk to you more about this, but not here. Tomorrow, at lunchtime, come to Peet's Coffee. Not the one next to us but the other one across town. Stop at your house first and wait for ten minutes. Look around when you come back to your car. Make sure no one is watching you," Seth instructs.

"Why all the cloak and dagger?" James asks.

"Tomorrow. Please do exactly as I ask," Seth replies cryptically. "So today is 'Q-Day.' I really never thought I would see it. Your place in history is set."

# CHAPTER 17

# THE PROPOSITION

James sits in his car in front of his house as instructed. He is staring at his watch to make sure to wait ten minutes. His facial tick is in overdrive. His hands are shaking. He is talking to himself.

"This is weird. Not part of the engineer's job description," he mutters out loud.

James looks up and down the street, scrutinizing a passing car in his rearview mirror until it disappears from sight. Unable to sit still any longer, he nervously drives off to Peet's Coffee.

James walks into Peet's Coffee and spots Seth in the furthest back corner, away from other patrons. He makes his way over, feeling the tension in the air.

"James, thanks for coming," Seth says quietly. "I need to be really clear about something. Every time we meet like this, it's going to be somewhere new. We never talk in the office, and we never talk near either of our cars. Trackers can be put on our cars and so can bugs. Don't ever carry a backpack or briefcase when we meet."

James, confused and anxious, listens intently. Seth continues, "I don't expect Alpheus to track either of us, but keep in mind that this is very big money we are talking about, and they are particularly worried about someone like you taking your knowledge and giving it or selling it to another company. I will probably hear about it if they decide to track people. Hell, I'm the guy they would probably ask to do the tracking. I hope they ask me to track you!"

"I still don't know what you are talking about. Am I in danger?" James asks, his voice trembling.

Seth leans in closer, lowering his voice further. "James, you don't understand the magnitude of your discovery. Everything in the world is going to change. A few people are going to have all the money in the world, and a bunch of other people are going to lose all their money. Several governments would happily kill a lot of people to have this capability."

James stares at Seth, stunned. "So why don't we meet with the bosses and figure it out?"

Seth's expression hardens. "Fuck the bosses. This is your idea, and you are the guy who needs to benefit, not Alpheus."

James and Seth stare at each other. Seth reaches out and puts his hand on James's shoulder.

"It's OK, James. Don't worry. This is not a half-baked idea. I have been preparing for this moment for a long time. I know what I am doing," Seth says with a half grin.

# CHAPTER 18

# TEMPTATION AND DOUBT

Later, they walk next to a serene lake, the tranquil setting a contrast to the tension between them. James is deep in thought, weighing the implications of what Seth is suggesting. James's uncomfortable posture reveals the gravity of their conversation as they walk.

"I signed a lot of nondisclosures and made a lot of agreements when I started," James says, hesitating.

"Fuck all that," Seth replies fiercely. "We are going to take your idea and get out of here. I'm going to make you wildly rich. I mean wildly."

"You are suggesting that I steal the idea?" James asks, still grappling with the enormity of the situation.

"For once in your life stop thinking about what other people think about you. Think about yourself and what you want. No one has ever taken care of you. It's time to take care of yourself. I am going to enable you to personally profit from your idea," Seth insists.

"This is the big one. You have always wanted to be recognized for the real value of your work. If you give this to Alpheus, they will just take it. You will be a footnote. I want you to be in charge of your own life and reap the benefits of your skill and talent. It's time for people to stop mistreating you and pushing you around. It's time for you to take control. I can help you," Seth continues with a reassuring grin.

A long pause follows as James processes Seth's words. Finally, he asks, "Assuming that I agree with you, what do you want me to do?"

Seth outlines the plan, his voice steady and persuasive. "I want you to figure out how to take enough equipment from work to make RSA breaking work on the outside. I have the authority to move equipment from one of our facilities to another. We will stage it in an intermediary location, and it will just happen to disappear. You need to tell me what we need."

"Are we really going to get away with this, or am I on a path to prison?" James asks, his anxiety evident.

"I have a very detailed plan. I have been thinking about it for a long time," Seth reassures him.

"I'm not so sure," James says as his face winces.

"Well, now we have met and talked. You are already kind of in this. If this blows up, we both go down hard. So, relax and listen to me before throwing this opportunity away," Seth replies, his expression hardening. "I know people who are ready to use your invention to take money from the Bank of England. No one will figure it out at first, but we can point to it as the success of your system," Seth continues.

"Putting this all together is going to be hard," James asserts.

"What you can tell people is that I have given you stuff to work on that you are not allowed to talk about. People here will believe that. I am already the mysterious guy that Alpheus keeps around and pays a bunch of money to," Seth explains.

"What's to stop your 'friends' from ratting us out?" James asks.

"For starters, they are going to get rich. You are only giving them one key, so it will only last for one job, but long enough to make them more money than they ever thought they would have. It's also really good for us because it shows the future customer that it's real. It's going to be about the biggest news story in the whole world. At first, they might believe that somebody on the inside gave information," Seth explains.

James nods slowly. "Well, like you said, I'm already sort of in this. I told you before that I would follow you anywhere. I'm in."

Seth smiles. "I'm glad you said that. I'm not really sure what I could have done if you said no."

# CHAPTER 19

# POINT OF NO RETURN

Seth and James stand at a distance from Seth's Porsche, parked in the corner of a church parking lot under a tree. Seth is dressed well, as usual, but in more casual clothes. They are 20 feet above a passing road, the parking lot clear for hundreds of feet in all directions. "You have liver cancer," Seth says bluntly. James looks at him, bewildered. "I do?" "According to Dr. Johansson," Seth replies.

"Never met him," James says, trying to grasp the situation.

"That's funny because he already has your biopsy, and it looks grim, buddy," Seth says, his tone serious.

Seth continues, "You are seriously going to disappear. Once we leave, you can never talk to anyone you know ever again. Anyone you talk to is going to get killed. If you let them know anything about you after that, you're going to get killed, too."

"I don't have anyone to talk to," James says with a gloomy look. He straightens and considers these words. The expression on his face shows that he knows this is the point of no return.

Seth replies, "I know. James, we are going to take care of each other. You are safe with me."

"How are you going to disappear?" James asks.

"I am going to take my planned sabbatical. I will just never come back," Seth explains.

James goes to the doctor whom Seth has arranged to fake his cancer diagnosis.

In the silent and sterile office, the doctor examines James. Seth's voice from their earlier conversation echoes in James's mind: "You are going to just not show up one day in two weeks. I need you to collect up all your data files and encrypt anything you leave behind."

James exits a taxi on a street corner, handing over cash to the driver. He walks with a sense of determination, his mind racing. Seth's voice continues in his head: "We are going to start a new life, but you will have absolutely everything you could ever dream of. Live out your days finding out just how much money one person can spend."

Seth approaches an older American car in a parking garage, his new ride.

# CHAPTER 20

# THE FINAL STEPS

A run-down hotel in San Jose has a battered door. The old American car that Seth picked up is parked a few spaces down. Inside the dark room with curtains drawn, James and Seth discuss the final steps of their plan.

"Once the bank heist is done, we are taking a lot of money and leaving the country. I have people who are going to facilitate our meetings with potential customers," Seth explains.

James looks uneasy. "This sounds a lot like selling nuclear secrets.

People get caught for that and go to jail forever, or they die."

"We just have to be smarter than the people getting caught. I'm pretty smart, James, and I really don't want to die. I want to blow ten million a year just fucking around," Seth says with infectious confidence.

James grins despite himself. "Why don't we just keep stealing money ourselves?"

"We would eventually be tracked down. We couldn't build enough power to make ourselves safe fast enough," Seth replies.

James sees now that Seth has been planning all this for a long time. He was just waiting for him to come along. He has been sucked in in steps. He's not sure if he is even angry about it. Seth is clearly in charge of his surroundings. He's a guy who sees what he wants and then grabs it. What does James have to lose? His close friends and family? His respect as a person and a professional? James thinks this might not be such a bad deal.

# CHAPTER 21
# THE HEIST

Over the next few months, James transfers equipment to a remote Alpheus storage space. He purchases copies of his lab equipment. It looks like he is just backing up his work. Meanwhile, Seth has teams removing the equipment and storing it in a private building.

Seth instructs James, "Use Uber to take you to a few blocks away from the safe house. Don't let anyone associate your car with the place. Make sure you get dropped off at a different place every time. Take a walk for exercise. Use a different route each time."

James spends the weekends reassembling his laboratory in the new building. It's in an industrial part of the city, so there are no questions asked. Seth is so much in control of purchases and equipment at Alpheus that no one is asking questions.

James also copies his computer contents and has an identical setup in the new building. He has duplicated his Alpheus lab and proven that it has the same capabilities. He spends so much time alone that no one has noticed his reduced overtime. James erases or encrypts everything on his Alpheus computer.

Sitting on a park bench next to a wide-open lawn and pond, Seth explains his plans to James. "I have collected gigabytes of encrypted messages sent between two Bank of England departments. I paid a guy to just keep saving messages in their transmitted form. At some point, they need to be in the open to be transmitted from one place to another. He has access to bank systems, but all account transactions are password-protected. I want you to take the encrypted content and break it."

"If I have enough content, I can do it. The computer will keep working until the unencrypted data looks like regular text. Once I accomplish that, though, next you need messages that give us the information we need to take money. Tell your guy to keep storing messages," James explains. "We need specifics of several accounts."

"Got it. He knows already, I think," Seth says. "I'm going to have my guy transfer 100 million pounds in pieces to a few individual accounts. Those guys are keeping a cut and transferring the rest to Bitcoin. He and they need to disappear quickly, but they will have the money to do it."

More weeks pass, and James cracks the bank messages. Seth has his plant continue to intercept messages. Finally, information for several large accounts is passed, and James gives the information to Seth. He instructs his plant to make the transfers and advises that he disappear quickly.

Adira notices that James is not working as much on weekends. One day, at the office, she takes Seth aside.

"James looks like he is actually living like a normal person and doing stuff on weekends. This is a big change. Do you think he's OK?" she asks.

"I told James to try a little work-life balance," Seth responds. "We don't want to burn him out. I encouraged online dating. That has to be taking a lot of his time now. Don't worry about James. He's OK."

Adira inquires, "They tell me you are going to take your sabbatical.

Where are you going, and what are you doing? Will I see you at all?"

Seth responds, "I'm going to help a friend start up a business. He has good ideas, but he's not a leader. I'll help him find people and set things up. I can teach him along the way. I'll probably also make a good bit of money. We agreed that I am going incommunicado while I do this. His customers are all potential, and I need to convince them to drop their usual suppliers. It's going to be controversial. Nothing new for me, of course."

"No. Nothing new. Secrecy and controversy. This has Seth written all over it," Adira responds with a grin.

"Well, wish me luck. Keep the ship sailing while I'm gone," Seth replies, also smiling.

Seth knows this is the last time he will talk to Adira. He considers this loss in his life. They had a relationship once. Though he was afraid to ever express such emotions to anyone in his life, Seth loved her. She was the closest Seth ever came to truly caring about another person. She is going to be sad when he disappears. That's the price of doing business. He needs to keep up appearances right to the end.

# CHAPTER 22

# THE MORNING UNFOLDS

Parvati stands in her small kitchen, the early morning light seeping through the dimly lit window. She pours breakfast cereal into a bowl at a small round table, her eyes fixed on the television. The news anchor's voice fills the room, their tone somber.

"Today it has been discovered that a hundred million pounds, which is about 122 million dollars, have been stolen from the Bank of England," the reporter announces. "Bank spokesmen have not been forthcoming on details, but inside sources have told us that a fundamental breach has occurred. A trusted system has been compromised."

Parvati's eyes widen. She sets the cereal box down, her mind racing. How could something like this happen? She has been working on quantum computing for years, and the thought that a quantum computer might be involved comes to her mind. Bank secrets are kept very secure, and even if they wanted to, one person could not single-handedly find and reveal enough information to perform an operation like this. There had to be an explanation about how such access was gained. Then she thinks of James disappearing from work. Could this be related? Parvati also thinks of all the people who must have been hurt by the disappearance of 122 million dollars. Is it people's life savings? Was it supposed to pay for schools? She decides to ask some questions at work.

Later that day, in a bustling Best Buy, a crowd gathers around a large television set. The news continues to blare, capturing the attention of everyone nearby. The title "US Secretary of Commerce" flashes across the screen.

"The breach of security at the Bank of England is a fundamental threat to international security," the secretary of commerce declares. "We will get to the bottom of this. I promise to protect you and secure our country."

A reporter steps forward, microphone in hand. "There's talk about this being related to quantum computing. Are we about to lose all encryption?

Are our markets going to fail?"

"There is no evidence that quantum computing was involved," the secretary assures. "This was a clever crime but a conventional crime. We know what to do. Several bank employees associated with the crime have disappeared."

A man watching the program thinks, "'We know what to do.' That's a load of shit." He looks at the others around him and thinks about what it means if all their bank accounts are emptied. He imagines chaos.

# CHAPTER 23

# A SAFE HAVEN

In a modest hotel in Ciudad Juarez, Mexico, James stands back while Seth checks in. James can hear Seth speak passable Spanish. Seth shakes his head at the attendant, waving a pile of cash. He slips a few extra bills across the counter. The attendant discreetly pockets them. Seth wanted a remote room and no disturbances. The attendant was initially uncomfortable without the usual showing of ID, but the extra cash let them pass.

They head to their room, shutting the door and drawing the curtains. Seth places a briefcase full of cash on the table alongside a blue steel Colt .45 pistol.

"What is our plan now?" James asks.

Seth leans back, a small smile playing on his lips. "Well, we are relatively safe for the moment here. We paid cash, and nobody knows us. No one saw us together. We should be able to stay anonymous as long as we keep moving. The next step is to talk to potential customers."

James frowns. "I really don't know how this is going to work. I think we might be pretty safe at the moment, but anybody we trust can give us up. How do you know we will not walk into a trap?"

Seth's eyes narrow. "It's a combination of trust and money. We took enough money to pay people very well. My friends are a little afraid of me, too. They don't really know what I am up to, but money is power, so they probably think that if they fuck me over, they might die. The guys who did the heist are gone. If they are lucky, no one will ever see them again."

"Who is the first customer?" James asks, a hint of apprehension in his voice.

"The Russians," Seth replies.

Seth has a Pelican case that he opens. It has a 75-centimeter VSAT terminal.

Seth explains, "All we need here is a laptop and this terminal. We will keep this with us for a while. If the heat is ever on, we dump it. With enough money, I can have anything delivered anywhere."

Seth unfolds the small satellite dish and points it from a balcony at the back of their small room. The antenna has an LED indicator showing when the dish is pointed at the satellite. He looks around to make sure no one can see him. He performs a few operations on a laptop.

"You don't need to do anything this time. I am just sending some information," Seth explains.

# CHAPTER 24

# THE SETUP

In a small, cluttered room in a Chicago warehouse, Fred and Robert move around purposefully. Ethernet cables dangle from the ceiling, and portable rack-mounted hardware sits on a central table. They are anonymous associates of Seth. He has paid them both to perform this operation. They know there is risk, and they both want to finish the job and leave as quickly as possible.

"How much time left?" Robert asks.

"Thirty minutes," Fred responds, glancing at his watch. "Where is the signal going?" Robert inquires.

"Russia," Fred says, his tone matter-of-fact.

Robert hesitates, a look of concern crossing his face. "Am I safe?" Fred stops and looks at him. "What do you mean?"

"I mean, am I safe?" Robert repeats.

"No one should catch us, and I'm not going to kill you, Bobby. I need you for the job, and as much as I'm paying you, you should just do what I say. I'm getting paid more than enough, too," Fred reassures him.

"So, who's paying?" Robert probes.

"Bitcoin never tells," Fred replies cryptically.

"Where is the SATCOM signal coming from?" Robert persists.

Fred shrugs. "I don't really know, and I'm not supposed to know. We were given an IP address to patch to. The incoming data is anonymized. Based on the forwarding IP address, I know this is going to Russia."

Robert shudders. "That sounds creepy and dangerous. Aren't we going to be questioned? I set up the PC to do the job. It's ready."

"We're going to make contact for about an hour, then we wipe out the virtual machine and trash all the hardware. That includes the SATCOM terminal. I paid for internet access under a false name. I found a company that doesn't do much checking. I paid for a one-year subscription, but like I said, we will use it for an hour," Fred explains.

"Who is this guy paying a hundred grand for a one-hour call?" Robert asks incredulously.

"Look, if you don't want the money, you can leave," Fred snaps. "The money is already spent," Robert mutters.

Fred and Robert scurry around for thirty minutes preparing the equipment. Robert is nervous. He thinks Fred is only pretending to be confident.

The SATCOM call initiates, and Robert verifies the data stream.

Fred monitors the computer screen showing data porting away to a Russian IP address. The men watch as data passes, tension thick in the air.

There is a SATCOM terminal on the roof with a skyward-facing dish antenna.

In twenty minutes, Fred's phone rings. "Shut it down," a voice commands.

Fred turns to Robert. "Gather up the gear. Leave the cables behind. I am leaving it to you to trash this stuff. Just get out of the building and drive away as fast as you can."

They quickly clear the room, Robert wheeling the rack case on a pallet jack. Fred climbs the stairs to the roof and stands next to the SATCOM terminal antenna. Fred spots two white vans pulling up in front of the building. Several people get out, looking determined. He sees Robert stepping into his truck down the street. Good. Robert is gone.

Fred lifts the SATCOM terminal, moves across the roof to the opposite side of the white vans, and drops the equipment next to a dumpster three floors below. It crashes to the ground, the satellite dish collapsing in a heap. He thinks, "I might drive past later to see if I can grab that stuff, but smashed is OK." He finds the fire escape and descends rapidly, pushing down the hinged steps on each floor.

Someone sees him doing this. Fred reaches the ground.

The observer confronts him. "What are you doing? There's no

fire."

"We have to test the system periodically. I'm just making sure it works," Fred lies smoothly, hurrying across the street and not looking back. He disappears around a corner, leaving the observer puzzled.

"I might get the terminal later," Fred mutters to himself.

# CHAPTER 25

# QUESTIONS

At Alpheus, Noam sees Adira. Since he is infatuated with her, he takes the opportunity to talk to her.

Noam addresses Adira nervously. "Adira, what's the story with James?

All I heard is that he has cancer."

Adira replies, "Yes, that's what I heard, too. I have not been able to reach him on his mobile number. I'm worried about him."

"You know, he has never told me anything about all the work he has been doing. For some reason, he has been secretive. I can't tell you anything about his progress. If he dies, we are pretty much screwed," Noam replies.

"Aren't you making progress yourself?" Adira asks.

"I am supposed to process qubit information. James was the guy talking to the qubits. I have been working on my part, but without him, I had nothing important to develop. Now he's gone completely," Noam replies.

"We have strict rules regarding privacy, especially when it comes to medical issues. There is only so much I can do to find out about him. I guess we just need to hope for the best," says Adira.

"OK, well, tell me if you find anything out, please," Noam requests. I also care about the guy." He puts his hand on Adira's shoulder and smiles. "Try to look like a hero. Maybe you can impress her," he thinks.

Adira smiles politely and holds very still, hoping that Noam will remove his hand.

Noam retracts his hand, then turns and walks down the hall. Adira pauses and thinks about how Seth is also suddenly gone. It seems a little too convenient that both guys could suddenly vanish with no means of contacting them directly. It's true that Alpheus has just taken two big hits.

# CHAPTER 26

# PLAYERS BEHIND THE CURTAIN

In a dark conference room in a covert Russian FSB field office in the Russian Consulate in Seattle, three men sit around a table. The room is illuminated by an old slide projector, casting an image of Seth Lawrence on the screen. Two men are dressed in plain American street clothes, and one wears a suit. All three are in their thirties and strikingly handsome. They speak in Russian. "The American sent a message that they are ready to sell us the information for fifteen billion dollars," the man in the suit states. "I want them to think they are getting the money right up until we take them." The slide projector clicks, and a new image of Seth appears.

"We have been investigating the background of Seth Lawrence," the first man in plain clothes explains. "He just left Alpheus claiming he was taking a sabbatical. We have the names of several former colleagues. We have interrogated a few so far. Those should lead to others. Wherever they went, they had to rely on someone here to keep things moving. They need communication and equipment. We also have a plant in the Seattle PD. Alpheus is looking for Seth Lawrence, and we learned that his partner is named James Cathcart. He also disappeared. We think James is the scientist who discovered the way to make quantum computing work. Alpheus isn't saying anything about it, but they are looking for Seth and James. If they have figured out what this is all about, it's as valuable to them as it is to us. If the police get any leads, we will learn about them. It's really just a matter of time."

The suited man's face hardens. "Do whatever you need to do to get information. I'm fine with your taking people. I think a lot of these people are criminals. Probably nobody cares if some of them disappear. We have had such orders before. This is extremely important. The results of success or failure are extreme. Whatever we need to do to succeed, it must be done."

The men all stare at each other.

# CHAPTER 27

# SALES PITCH

Seth and James prepare for their next move. Seth sits by the door, his Colt .45 on the table in front of him. A mobile phone plays loud music from the bathroom to mask their speech. James sits at a laptop, the glow illuminating his tired, anxious face. Seth looks tired and scared, too. He stands behind James, peering at the laptop.

"OK, James. We sent your Alpheus demo video to the Russians. They also know about the bank heist," Seth says.

A cartoon display fills the laptop screen as Seth talks. "I made a little video for you. The handoff was a friend of a friend of a friend," he continues. The arrows on the map show data moving from Mexico to the US and then to Russia. The node in the US then becomes a puff of smoke.

"Some cops or feds showed up at the building. In ten more minutes, they would have been caught," Seth says and continues, "I'm right to stay on my toes. Even if they were caught, they can't identify us or tell anyone where we are. We will not be working with that team again. I trashed the SIM with the phone number I used to talk to them. That's how we stay safe. We're not going to pay the subscription on the SATCOM account, so it will die. Likewise with the VPN subscription. I doubt anyone can connect this to us personally other than to know already which five companies in the US have a fighting chance to make anything work. We are logged into a VPN from a virtual machine created on a new PC with a new internet subscription. We will wipe out the virtual machine and trash the PC when this is over."

Seth continues standing over James, who is wearing a headset with a microphone. "You will sit in front of a computer and a microphone, but they only see an avatar," Seth instructs. "You do need to be careful about what you say. This is live, so you can fuck yourself over in two seconds. It would take them a couple days to get here, but if we blow this place, we will need to pick a new country and lose a potential customer. I expect that their guy will have the job of trying to learn who you are and where you are. He might not even be that technical. He's probably GRU. He's a pro. If you get nervous about something, there is a big red button in front of you. Press it, and we go offline temporarily. You and I can talk and then rejoin the conversation. I told them that they need to be patient and that we have difficulties with our connection. That's bullshit, of course."

James nods, his anxiety palpable. "How do we have a connection now if your guys almost got caught?"

Seth explains, "I have a new team working. Same setup, different place. I tell them which satellite to use, and they set up the virtual machine and VPN. Our cutout arranges a meeting. We can use a guy a few times, but we don't maintain contact for long. I know about fifty people I can call to do jobs. They have their own contacts that I don't even know. The best way to do this is to have my guy hire a team and give them instructions. Then they don't even know me."

James looks very nervous. "I'm not going to hesitate to press the button.

I'd rather be safe than sorry."

"Good. That's how I want you to feel. The Russians know a hundred million pounds have been stolen. I told them it was our system. I told them the cost for the system is fifteen billion dollars," Seth says and continues, "They will certainly try to play games to fuck us over. Their top goal will be to figure out who we are and come get us so they can pay nothing. I'm going to have a red button, too. If I see things going wrong, I will punch you out. What I need you to do is prove to them that you made the breakthrough that makes this thing work without revealing too much. They know about the bank heist. Real money disappeared. The Russians have scientists who can tell it's legit. Without goods in hand, we can't ask for full market value. You know it's trillions. I think fifteen billion is enough to have a royal life forever."

James looks worried. "Seth, I am really scared. These people are known to kill. We are standing between them and a prime national goal. They are going to try as hard as they can to find us and torture us for the information."

Seth's expression hardens. "What you have saving you is that you are the one man with the knowledge worth trillions of dollars and world control. If they catch you, they will feed you and care for you until you give them the secret. Me, they will kill in two seconds. You might actually live to tell the tale."

There is a knock at the door. Seth leaps up and grabs and cocks his pistol. "Quien es?" Seth says in a loud voice, holding up his pistol.

"Solo la ama de llaves," a timid voice responds. It is a housekeeper. "No ahora por favor," Seth says in a calmer voice.

"Bien. Volveré más tarde," replies the voice. She will return later. "Bien. Gracias," Seth replies.

Seth lowers his pistol and turns to James. "We need to be ready for stuff like this. We will never know when it is something serious. We always need a way out and a plan. Right now, all we have is that window to jump out of."

# Chapter 28

# The Russians

James is in front of his laptop. He is nervous, and his shoulder twitches. His face winces. He is grateful to have an avatar hiding his true state. The laptop makes an alarm sound, and the screen temporarily goes dark. James straightens in his seat and looks at his avatar. Seth turns to look at the laptop, too. A well-dressed Russian man with facial hair appears on the screen in front of a brightly lit plain wall. He is also wearing a headset. He looks to be in his forties.

"Hello. I am Sergei. Let me congratulate you on your successful demonstration of quantum computing. You must be a very smart man. We respect you and value your ability. We want to meet with you to discuss this in detail. Also, you don't need this avatar. We would rather see your face to better understand you and so that we can build trust."

"That's not possible," James says.

Sergei says, "It is not clear to our scientists that you can just tell us something and it will start working."

James replies, "Well, it's your choice. We have plenty of interested parties. Whoever pays will get the secrets."

Sergei continues, "If we could meet, all doubts could be eliminated, and we would gladly pay your price."

James retorts, "Honestly, Sergei, if we meet, we will be taken hostage and never see any money. Like you said, I'm smart. This will be done strictly remotely. You and I will never meet face to face."

Sergei replies, "Oh, I already know your name, James Cathcart. We know exactly who you are. You can't escape us."

James hits the red button and turns to Seth in alarm. "Fuck! That was fast. How do they know?"

Seth replies, "I'm not sure. It was going to come out publicly at some point. The real question is how they can use that against us. I think we are safe for now."

James shivers, trying to control his fear. "What should I do?" "Let me take over for a minute," Seth says, switching the avatars.

He confronts Sergei on the screen. "Sergei, congratulations on your detective work. You do realize that this changes nothing. We have the knowledge, and you want it. If you fuck with us, we can hand it over to the Chinese in an hour. You can lose this whole game just by making threats. Even if you can locate us physically, we already have failsafe measures in place. Your worst nightmare is the Americans having the secret. If I press a button, everything is sent to the American government. It's like your nuclear threat. Fuck with us even a little bit, and you're done. I physically carry a box with a button. You fuck with me, and you're done."

Sergei's face remains impassive. "Fine. We need further demonstration before we give you anything."

Seth smirks. "The Bank of England has lost a hundred million pounds. We enabled decryption, and some friends of mine have walked away with some of the money."

"That is impressive," Sergei admits.

"Damn right. You know the price. Fifteen billion dollars," Seth retorts, ending the call.

James shuts the laptop and unplugs the Ethernet cable. "Do you really have a box with a button?"

"No. I was bullshitting them," Seth admits. "Maybe we should do that," James suggests.

"Look, if they get us, we're dead. They will kill us just because they're mad. You can press a button all you want."

"This is pretty fucked up," James mutters. "If they know who I am, they know who you are, and they know who we know. Now everyone who knows us is in danger."

"Relax. I thought this through. There are no surprises. Just keep your head on straight. You're in it now, brother. There is no turning back. What protects the people we know is that they don't know anything," Seth replies. "There is no information to be obtained."

James nods, trying to steady his nerves. "I guess so."

"Don't worry. I know about these guys. I told you they would try to trick you. I'm glad you pushed the button. The other guys are fucked up in different ways. Just wait until you meet the North Koreans," Seth says with a grim smile.

"Can they even speak English?" James asks.

"That's the scary part. They will have a guy who speaks perfect English. He was taken, kidnapped as a young person from a normal life somewhere else," Seth explains, his tone dark.

"Get ready to go. We are moving on," Seth instructs. "The housekeeper is going to find an empty room."

The room falls silent as they contemplate the dangerous path they have chosen.

# CHAPTER 29

# SEATTLE PD

Three officers sit around a small conference table in an old room in an old building.

"We are working with a company called Alpheus. They have two missing workers, and the company suspects some funny business," says the first officer.

"What is the funny business?" asks the second officer.

"The company guy just told us that it involves a corporate secret. The first guy, James Cathcart, claimed to have a cancer diagnosis and left work. He stuck around for two weeks, but it looks like all he was doing was clearing out his lab and erasing his data. After that, no one can reach him or knows where he is. He is apparently quite the loner, so we don't have family or friends to ask. He is just gone. The other guy is named Seth Lawrence. He is high up in the company. He does have friends, but no one knows where to find him either. He claimed he was taking a sabbatical, but he never arrived anywhere else. He is just gone," the first officer reports.

"What do we know about their whereabouts?" asks the third officer. "Seth was renting a car, which should have been a red flag. He usually drives awesome sports cars, but this thing was a second-rate American junker. It was found in Los Angeles, abandoned," continues the first officer. "If they were together, they appear to have been headed south."

"Neither have made any known contact since leaving?" the third officer inquires.

"Seth was apparently pretty well-connected. He's the kind of guy who talks to other guys who don't talk about it. Nobody is going to volunteer anything," the first officer continues.

"Have you found and questioned any of his associates?" asks the third officer.

"We talked to his known colleagues at work. One said he thought Seth was smiling too much. That doesn't really help us," the first officer reports.

"We have been keeping an eye on that guy. We have a warrant for a wiretap. We are listening to who he talks to. He uses Signal and WhatsApp, so we can't see any of his encrypted messages. We can see who he calls, though. To be honest, if he was doing anything sneaky, he would not do it in the open. Another person named Adira is reportedly pretty close to Seth. One guy said they had a thing once. We are watching her, too. If Seth contacts anyone, it might be her."

The meeting breaks up, and the first two officers leave.

The third officer looks around his desk to make sure no one is looking his way. It's close to lunchtime, so he walks out. He drives through a security gate and waves to the guard. He drives two miles down the road and pulls over. Under the passenger seat is a small black mobile phone. His normal phone is sitting on the passenger seat, so the black phone is obviously an extra. He looks in his rearview mirror and manually dials a number.

"There is a person named Adira who you need to pick up. The PD thinks she is the most likely contact for Seth. Other than that, they don't know anything we don't know," the officer says into the phone. He hangs up and hides it under his passenger seat. He drives on to a fast food restaurant, noting the time so that he can be back after a normal interval.

# CHAPTER 30

# THE NEXT STEP

In a cluttered hotel room in Ciudad Juárez, Mexico, Seth and James strategize. Empty food containers litter the floor and furniture.

"The North Koreans are a mixed bag," Seth begins. "On one hand, they might pay the most because they want to sidestep national destruction. On the other hand, they are definitely the most dangerous. Their spokesman is going to be a trip. He will certainly be other than Korean. He might be a Japanese guy they kidnapped as a teenager. By now, he has lived a full life of being a front man for the regime. He has probably lived in luxury, but he also knows they will kill him at the drop of a hat. Any attempted tricks will be scripted, so probably easier to spot. Just play it like you did with the Russians. Hit the big red button if it gets dicey."

James looks skeptical. "What is our goal?"

"Our goal is fifteen billion. Same as the Russians," Seth replies confidently. "They were sent your demo video, and they know the price."

"Should I sweeten it with any more information?" James asks.

Seth nods. "Hint at the nature of the breakthrough. The North Koreans are not as sophisticated as the Russians. You have less risk of giving anything away."

"I'll tell them that the secret is a new way to interrogate the spin state without destroying it," James says, bracing himself.

Seth once again unfolds a small VSAT terminal. He keeps it inside the room since the sky view in the right direction is unobstructed on a balcony.

The laptop dings and the screen goes dark momentarily. James's avatar, a cartoonish man with blonde hair, appears in the top right corner. A beautiful Asian woman appears on the screen. She is not Korean. She has darker skin. She wears a slim, formal dress, her hair tied above her head, exuding an air of deceptive innocence.

"Hello. My name is Samantha," she introduces herself.

James raises an eyebrow. "You are not who I expected to meet."

"Who did you expect?" Samantha asks.

"For one thing, you're not Korean," James replies.

Samantha smiles coyly. "Does it matter? So long as I have the money." "Well, that's true. Let's talk about doing business," James concedes.

"We are prepared to pay you, but we need proof that what you have works. We have scientists who can evaluate what you have to sell," Samantha states.

James shakes his head. "I will not be sending you any details. My proof is the hundred-million-pound acquisition from the Bank of England."

"If we could meet with you to ask questions, we would be more comfortable giving you the large amount of money that you have asked for," Samantha suggests.

James scoffs. "If you meet me, Samantha, and I am sure I would never meet you in person, I will end up in chains with a hot poker up my ass. This needs to be a completely remote arrangement."

James thinks about how his confidence is increasing. This life on the run is turning him into a new person.

Samantha's smile fades. "Then we need more information to evaluate your proposal."

"You can take what I offer or watch someone else get it. I'm not interested in being cheated or tortured. The choice is yours," James retorts.

Samantha tries a different tactic. "We can offer half of the money. Then we evaluate what you have, and we pay you the rest."

James is unmoved. "That guarantees that I will only ever see half of the money. I am also not interested in that. Unless half of the money is fifteen billion dollars."

Samantha's patience thins. "I must have more information to deliver to the people who will decide."

"Tell them that quantum computing depends entirely on modifying, maintaining, and measuring quantum states. I have personally determined how to make the required measurement without simultaneously destroying the state. That is what stops everyone else. This is what I offer," James explains.

Samantha nods curtly. "Then we are done communicating for now. I will be in touch."

"You have one week to decide. If you don't respond, we will go to another customer," James warns.

"Who is your other customer?" Samantha probes.

"That is not relevant to our deal," James says, pressing the red button to end the call. He shuts down the laptop, pulls the Ethernet plug, and closes the lid.

"That was a curveball. Maybe they think I will believe I can get laid in this deal," James muses aloud.

Seth chuckles. "I suggest dating someone else. That was good. Throwing a hot woman into the equation is unexpected but not surprising. You were looking at a lifelong North Korean agent. She would cut your throat with her own hands."

James sighs. "We should talk carefully about what exactly I should tell them."

"We can talk more about that. We have worn out our welcome here," Seth asserts. "It's time to move on again."

# CHAPTER 31

# DARK DEALINGS

In a shaCk on a remote farm in California, Adira sits handcuffed to a wooden chair. Her face is bruised, her nose bleeding, and one eye swollen dark purple. Two men sit across from her, a pistol lying ominously on the table between them. A bright light shines directly into Adira's eyes, making the large men appear even more menacing.

"We aren't the cops, and we aren't the government," the larger man says. "We are two guys who want information, and we can do whatever we want to you. No one knows you are here, and no one will know when you die. We know you are involved with Seth Lawrence. We don't give a shit about you. The only reason you are alive right now is that we want to know something you know."

Adira's voice trembles. "But if I tell you anything, what's to stop you from killing me?"

The second man grins. "Well, maybe we will be glad that you told us and let you go. Tell us where Seth Lawrence is."

Adira thinks about Seth. They were once together. Seth never told her that he loved her, but Adira knew deep down that he cared for her. As professionals, they both had serious goals, and they decided to proceed as friends and associates rather than lovers. Still, he was important to her, and she also felt love for him.

Adira thinks of happier days. He has brought her to this fate. It's his fault.

She wants to protect him, but she is also angry.

"Seth disappeared. We have not seen him for weeks. He is not in contact with anyone. I can't help you, so I guess that's it," Adira says plaintively.

"I'm not going to kill you now, but we are going to hold you. Maybe Seth will want to save you," says the menacing man. "We know you were fucking him."

Adira is shocked and horrified that they know so much about her. Seth will not know she is being held. She wonders if he would care enough to do something.

# CHAPTER 32

# AN UNCERTAIN FUTURE

James and Seth drive down Mexico's Highway 85 in a large SUV. Seth grips the wheel tightly, his eyes scanning the road ahead.

In a dingy hotel room in Mérida, Mexico, Seth still has a pistol, but it is in a holster on his side. The drapes are slightly open to let in a little light, but the room lights are turned off. A mobile phone is playing loud music in the bathroom again.

The rear window faces the sky. Seth has it wide open with the VSAT terminal on a small table facing skyward. Again, the terminal is inside the room as its angle allows a view of the sky in the right direction to communicate with the satellite.

James looks at Seth, curiosity etched on his face. "What do you want from all of this?"

Seth's eyes gleam with desire. "I want to tell them the exact kind of girl I want to fuck. She can look like anything I want, talk like I want, and do what I want. Whatever I ask for, they will get it for me. Money buys everything. I mean everything."

James shakes his head, a wistful smile on his lips. "Man, I just want a cool car."

Seth laughs. "Well, you name it. They will bring you what you want. They will give you a racetrack if you want it. These guys already do everything they want."

James's smile fades. "I guess we need to really disappear."

Seth's tone turns serious. "I am telling you in all seriousness. If you ever, I mean ever, contact anyone you know, it will all end. They will be hurt, and you will be hurt. For the rest of your life, you need to follow the rules. Just have a party and stop thinking about anything you used to care about. Work out and have a private chef make every meal. Fuck a different girl every night. Drive ten cars. Buy thousand-dollar bottles of wine. Try some drugs."

James still wonders if he has done the right thing. Seth is an extreme guy and seems reckless. It's true, though; there is no turning back now.

"OK, man. Take it easy," James mutters, glancing at the laptop.

Seth looks at James with a serious expression. "If someone comes to the door, we go out that window. Run for a while. We can separate. We can carefully approach the car a little later. I'm ready to go."

This time, Seth is sitting in front of the laptop. James says to Seth, "The laptop is ready. You're on."

The laptop alarms and goes momentarily dark. Seth's avatar appears in the top right corner. Sergei, well-dressed, like he was at their last meeting, appears on the screen.

"You are not James," Sergei states. "I mean, all I see is your stupid avatar."

"Does it matter?" Seth replies nonchalantly.

"Not at all. We know who you are, too," Sergei threatens. "If this is Seth, you should know that we have Adira."

Seth presses the red button. He rocks back and places his hand on his forehead.

"Fuck. These guys are getting too close," Seth says. He tries to regain his composure. Showing any weakness will only make things worse. He reestablishes the connection.

"Threaten all you want. Sergei, you saw what we could accomplish. We hacked a bank and took a lot of money. Who has ever been able to do that? The technology is proven, and it's infinitely expandable. From here out, it's just engineering and money. You can make as big a computer as you want, and you can solve any problem," Seth explains.

Sergei nods. "Yes, you did prove that you could make something work. We want it. We just can't give you billions of dollars without being sure that we will get what we want."

Seth's tone hardens. "Yeah, well, we can't fucking meet you and think we will not end up chained to a wall with electric wires on our balls. You have to do this our way. I want you to pay in Bitcoin. You pass me the QR codes, and I confirm the contents. I'm going to cash some to make sure it's real. When we confirm that half of the money is in the accounts, we tell you about the technology. When the rest is in, we send you details. Drawings and documents. We will tell you everything about the hack that we already accomplished."

Sergei's face remains stoic on the screen. "How do I know that we will not send you seven and a half billion and watch it disappear for nothing?"

Seth leans forward, his tone icy. "Well, to some extent, you have to take a chance. Your other option is to watch the US make this work and eat your lunch. I'm handing you the keys to controlling the world. I think my price is pretty damn cheap. You can steal a billion in a few weeks."

Sergei's eyes narrow. "If you fuck us over, you better be really good at hiding. We will find you, and you will regret this in the worst way."

Seth smirks. "Oh, we're pretty fucking good at hiding."

With that, Seth terminates the call, turns off the laptop, and unplugs the Ethernet connector. He looks over at James, who is fidgeting anxiously.

"We're OK. They can't find us right now," Seth assures him.

He pushes a table and couch against the only door in the room. They are on the third floor, so he opens another window for more air. Seth places the Colt .45 on the nightstand next to him and switches off the light. Moonlight fills the room, enough to see James's wide-eyed expression.

"They have Adira. That's really, really bad," James says.

"I know. She doesn't know where we are. She can't tell them anything that can hurt us," Seth replies.

"I don't know the details, but it's pretty obvious that you care about each other," James says. "I see how you talk to each other and look at each other."

"I do care about her, but if they have her, indicating any concern is going to make things a lot worse. I need to pretend I don't care," Seth explains.

"They might kill her," James says with a worried expression.

"They might. What is protecting her is that she has nothing to tell them. If I don't contact her, she can't be a tool. I think they will hold her for a while and hopefully let her go," Seth says.

"So, the Russians know my name and your name. That means they know what we look like. If they have any idea at all where we are, they can try to find us," James says, looking even more concerned.

"I agree with you. We have been very careful, and we need to keep it up.

We will not stay here for long," Seth assures. "Just one night."

# CHAPTER 33

# A NEW DAY, A NEW DEAL

Early the next morning, a watch alarm wakes Seth. He makes a quick, animated phone call before James wakes up.

"James, get ready," Seth commands. "The Russians shook us up, but we need to stay focused. Next, we are talking to the Chinese. A new team in a new state set this up. They have the demo."

Without a word, James heads to the bathroom. The sound of the shower running fills the room. Seth inspects the Colt, racking it a few times to cycle three bullets. He then removes the magazine and puts the bullets back in.

The Russians have Adira. This is not going to go well. If they have abducted her, there's no way they are going to release her. It's a one-way ticket. Seth decides he's going to try to save her. He did love her, and he wants her to be alive and happy. This penetrates his tough persona. He needs to do the right thing. He's not going to tell James. This is breaking all the rules. James is showering, so Seth picks up his phone. This is a fresh SIM card, but every call to the US draws attention.

Seth calls Fred in Chicago.

"Hello. Who is this?" Fred answers. "This is Seth."

"What? I'm not supposed to hear from you. Why are you calling?" Fred inquires.

"Some Russian guys grabbed Adira. I need you to find her," Seth says. "How am I supposed to find her, and what am I supposed to do? Shoot them all? I'm in Chicago. Do you even think she is in Seattle? What do you want from me?" Fred asks.

"You are a fixer. I want you to find someone who can shoot them. I want you to find a detective and give him Adira's description and tell them the name Sergei. We have to try to find her. They will kill her," Seth implores. "If you find her, send her to Istanbul. Her whole life is blown. She has to get out."

"Istanbul. Is that where you are?" Fred asks.

"No, I have contacts there," Seth lies. Shit. He usually isn't this sloppy. "Just get this done. I am transferring double your money to your account."

"I'll do my best. If I find her, I will turn the flag red on that website we agreed on," Fred explains.

"Please watch your back. If these guys grabbed Adira, they could grab you. They are killers," Seth warns. "That's all you need to know. Just try to save her."

Seth hangs up. What if she does come to Istanbul? What a life that could be. Fucking a new girl every night was probably going to be a dead end. Seth never let Adira get any closer than sex, but maybe she's worth the risk. He can't let James know he has done this. He has just broken every rule he laid down for James.

James returns, dressed in sweats.

"OK. Just concentrate. Same rules," Seth instructs. "OK. Got it. Ready," James responds.

Seth enters a new IP address into the laptop while checking his phone notepad. James takes his position. The screen goes momentarily blank before James's avatar appears in the top right corner. A black-haired Chinese man in his fifties appears on the screen.

"I am Liu Jianguo. I want to talk to you about purchasing your discovery," the man introduces himself.

"You're a little late to the game. We have bids already," James says, trying to sound confident.

Seth smiles and nods at James.

"What are your bids? Perhaps we can do better," Jianguo inquires. "We are considering a bid for fifteen billion," James replies.

"Whoever made that bid is lying to you. They want to trick you and kill you," Jianguo warns.

James remains calm. "I think everyone wants to trick us and kill us. We know how to get the money and escape. We have several fail-safe plans. At a minimum, we can always just give it to the Americans in a second with the press of a button."

"We can protect you and give you a place to go when you sell. The Americans will be out to get you," Jianguo offers.

"We have our own plans. We just want the money," James insists.

Jianguo sighs. "We can't pay you fifteen billion dollars without knowing that we are getting a working system. I want us to come to a deal. What if we give you five billion and the rest once we know it works?"

James shakes his head. "That means I will get five billion and never see you again. Until next time, my friend."

James turns off the laptop. Seth is already pulling on a light jacket.

"You did a good job. I doubt the Chinese will be our customer. It was worth a try. The bottom line is that we need to get our hands on the most money possible and disappear. Put on your travel clothes; we are moving on," Seth instructs. "We are moving on big time."

A close-up of James's face shows how nervous he is, his face twitching. In a strange way, James is getting used to this life. He has done the pitch several times now. James just hopes Seth has really thought through their safety because he now has no control.

# CHAPTER 34

# THE END OF THE LINE

Adera sits alone in a small, locked room. She has been here for more than a week. Boredom is the worst torture. There are only so many sit-ups a person can do. Suddenly, she hears the door unlocking. A handsome young man in street clothes comes into the room. He is holding a pistol.

The man stands admiring Adira. She is certainly beautiful. What a shame. "We would like to know if you are ready to tell us where to find Seth

Lawrence," the man says.

"I told you before, I don't know where he is. I don't know what I can do for you," Adira responds.

"Your usefulness to us depends on information. The end of your usefulness is also the end of your life, you understand?" the man threatens.

"Well, you want me enough to keep me in this box for a week," Adira responds.

The man pistol whips her face. Blood spurts from her cheek near her eye.

She grasps her face with her hands and falls to the ground.

"I will keep you just as long as I think you might be useful. That's it," the man says roughly.

"God. How many times can I tell you? Seth didn't tell me his plans, and he didn't contact me. He just disappeared. I know as little as anyone else about where he is," Adira sobs, holding her face.

"If you have nothing to offer to me, I have nothing to offer to you," the man says, raising his pistol.

Adira closes her eyes and covers her face. The man steps forward, points at her head, and shoots her dead. He calmly leaves the room.

# CHAPTER 35

# A YACHT AND A JOURNEY

Seth parks their SUV behind some trees in an open field near Mérida Port. They ditched the VSAT terminal, so all they carry are bags with clothes and cash. That and Seth's pistol. They head towards a 50-foot yacht docked nearby, standing out among the much less impressive boats in the harbor. Seth puts his arm around James as they walk towards the dock.

"Do you care who gets it and what they do with it?" James asks, breaking the silence.

"No," Seth replies bluntly.

James looks troubled. "Some people are definitely going to get hurt."

As they walk through the open field, Seth sighs and begins to share his story. "Let me explain something to you. I was the son of a diplomat. We lived in many countries. I hardly ever saw my father due to his work, and I managed to get in trouble with local kids wherever we went. In Iraq, my father uncovered a plan that Saddam Hussein wanted to purchase high explosives from North Korea. To try to keep the story under wraps, the Iraqis imprisoned him over a scandal involving a made-up affair with an Iraqi diplomat's wife.

Normally, the US government would have fought for his freedom, but his accusation that they were trying to buy conventional weapons did not fit the WMD narrative, and George W. Bush wanted to start a war. As soon as the war started, the Iraqis killed my father in jail. That was 2003. I hate the US government for abandoning my father to death just for their political purposes. To some extent, I have found that big corporations are just the same. They will let you die to get what they want. If we don't take care of ourselves, no one will."

Seth takes out his pistol, turning it over in his hands. "I was eighteen years old. Now I'm thirty-eight. Since I was eighteen, I have dabbled in some questionable business adventures and generally skirted the law to make money. Since 2003, I have been looking for a chance to stick it to the USG. So, who's going to get hurt? Big companies? Governments? Fuck 'em. Next stop, Santo Domingo, Puerto Rico. It should take us four or five days to get there. This should be about the safest we have been for a while. I can check to see who has tried to contact us since yesterday, but for a few days, we are going offline."

James looks at Seth with new admiration. "Seth, I'm sorry. Things make a lot more sense. I am going to help you."

Seth considers his own wretched story. Instead of letting it keep him down, Seth has aggressively pursued everything he wants. He feels like he is finally going to have it all. He smiles at James. "Thanks, buddy."

# CHAPTER 36

# SAFE AT SEA

Seth and James sit on the deck of the 50-foot yacht, sipping drinks under a small, shaded structure. The day is bright and hot, the sea calm. A portly, middle- aged bearded man is at the controls upstairs.

"Unless a pirate ship roars up, we are clear of everything dangerous," Seth says confidently.

James takes a deep breath. "I have had some time to think about what is going to happen when the Russians or Koreans or Chinese release quantum computing on the world. None of them plan to do anything reasonable or sensible. I think they are all going to try their best to destroy everyone else. I don't think you are considering the fact that if they destroy the world, it will no longer be a nice place to live in."

Seth nods thoughtfully. "You understand this better than I. I do understand that when encryption fails, a lot of things are going to break. No one is prepared. I guess no one really ever thought this could actually happen, at least not anytime soon. You certainly surprised me. Your discovery is amazing. We are not going to be living in the world. I for one do not plan to spend a lot of time finding out what's happening."

"It's just too bad that something that could solve so many problems is going to cause problems instead," James laments. "We could have used this to solve important problems that would make everyone's life a lot better. Instead, we are selling it to animals bent on destruction. Unfortunately, the guy who wants to cure diseases and simulate impossibly complicated physical systems doesn't have fifteen billion dollars to give us. The world will very quickly need to find new ways to encrypt information. At first, we will be back to the dark ages. If you want to pass information, you need to have a guy physically go somewhere and tell someone a secret. They can also use World War II technology. Code books and one-time pads will work. Again, it's security through physical isolation. Don't involve any computers. They will eventually implement what people are calling 'Post-Quantum

Cryptography.' The PQC algorithms are created using mathematical problems that no known conventional or quantum algorithm can solve. One is called 'Lattice-based Cryptography.' Things will eventually go back to normal, but in addition to the near-term problem of having no security for your bank account, the 'Harvest Now, Decrypt Later' idea means that the people who get the secret will decrypt all the data from their adversaries that they have been storing for years. It's hard to even guess the fallout."

Seth leans back, taking a sip of his drink. "I care less than you, and I am probably thinking more about my future excesses, but you're right. There are going to be some very serious problems. I think this is analogous to nuclear weapons. It was a new technology that someone figured out. In that case, it didn't turn everything upside-down, but it did change the world. I just couldn't stomach handing this over to Alpheus. If it wasn't you, someone would have made it work eventually. You and I are just taking advantage of an important situation. We know what's going to happen, and we are taking care of ourselves first. Otherwise, you would have watched other people make trillions of dollars while you lived out your average life."

James nods in agreement. "I do understand, and I am glad you showed up. There's a lot I didn't know. I was really used to doing great things and not being appreciated for it. People always took my stuff and passed me by. I have my own anger here, too. You are not the only one who is glad to stick it to somebody. Please just try to make us rich and not dead."

"Señor, how much longer?" Seth asks the captain.

"We will be there in three hours. Todo está bien," the captain assures. The sea journey concludes successfully. James and Seth land in Puerto Rico.

# CHAPTER 37

# BACK AT HOME

Charles, Parvati, and Noam sit around a small table at the Alpheus coffee shop. "There is some seriously weird shit going on," Charles says.

"No kidding. James is gone, Seth is gone, and Adira is gone. These people are all related," Noam replies.

"Yes, and the news about the bank heist seems related. Some people are asking if quantum computing might be involved. I think it is, and I think we know who it is," Parvati asserts.

"I don't know who to talk to, but this is management territory. We were close to these people, and we should be informed," Charles replies.

"Phillip and Alfred are two managers on this project. I am going to talk to them," Parvati says.

Parvati calls a meeting with Phillip and Alfred, meeting them in a small conference room.

"Gentlemen, I must tell you that the quantum computing team is in a bit of turmoil. We have lost three of our most important people, and we are also suspicious," Parvati declares.

"Parvati, you are right to be concerned. We are concerned, too. We are in contact with the Seattle PD. We are looking for James and Seth and Adira. We are aware of your concerns," Phillip explains.

"I think the fact that James and Seth were directly involved with quantum computing and that the hundred-million-pound Bank of England heist might involve quantum computing are related. I think this is all extremely serious," Parvati asserts.

"Believe me, that has occurred to us. We want to find these people. Not only do we have questions, but they can all be in danger," Alfred adds.

"I know HIPA means you can't ask questions about a person's medical issues, but where is James?" Parvati asks.

"James is gone. Seth is gone. Adira is gone. We can't find any of them. Forget HIPA. We know James's disappearance has nothing to do with cancer," Phillip explains.

"So, what, we just wait around until someone grabs more of us?" Parvati doesn't meet his eyes but picks at the lid of her empty drink.

"We think James discovered something and Seth took him away. I don't think the rest of you are in danger. Adira was close to Seth, so either she is with him, or she is in hiding," Phillip continues.

"Well, I'm going to watch my ass. This is scary," Parvati says.

"Do be careful. Tell your team we are working on it," Phillip states.

It's early evening when Ethan walks to his car in the Alpheus parking lot. Just as he opens his door, he notices a man standing near the trees at the edge of the lot. The man puts a phone to his head as he looks at Ethan. Ethan is aware of the situation with James and Seth, and this alarms him. He rushes into his car and starts it.

"I never liked that new guy," Ethan thinks. "Or Seth."

Ethan drives out of the parking lot. He's had a long workday, and he's looking forward to going home. Crossing an intersection, he notices a person sitting in a parked car, unmoving. Is this guy watching him? "Come get some, fuckers," Ethan thinks. He is pretty sure he can defend himself just fine. He takes a few turns heading towards his apartment.

Ethan parks his car and walks down a narrow alley that leads to the front of the building. As he nears the street, a man steps out in front of him.

"Ethan, I need you to meet a few people who want to talk to you," the man says.

"I'm not going anywhere with anyone," Ethan growls, standing in a defensive position.

The man shoots Ethan with a taser, and Ethan's twitching body collapses to the ground. Two more men come around the corner. One injects Ethan in the leg, and he passes out.

Sometime later, he opens his eyes. He is in a dark room with a bright light shining in his face. A man he can't see starts talking. His vision and hearing are still affected by the drug he was injected with.

"Ethan, we want to talk to you about James and Seth. We want to know where they are. We know you work with them," the faceless man says.

"I worked for that piece of shit James, but I have no idea where they are," Ethan replies, tugging at his restraints.

"I think you know something. You were close to James. He must have told you things," the man replies.

"James didn't tell me shit, and if he did, fuck you. I won't tell you anything," Ethan sneers.

The man emerges from the darkness and punches Ethan hard in the face. Blood splashes from his nose and mouth. The man hits him several more times, his leather gloves breaking Ethan's skin.

"See, it's not really like that. Instead, you are going to fucking do whatever the fuck I tell you right now, or you are going to die. I'm ready to kill you right this minute," the man says. Ethan can see his face. He is tall and muscular. He has a strangely large head.

"Fuck. OK. James has cancer. He is gone from work. Seth took a sabbatical. I don't talk to them, and I don't know where they are," Ethan says sheepishly. He is bleeding a lot.

"That's what they said, but everyone in your company knows they stole something. We think you talk to James. We need to find him," the large man replies.

"If I can get myself out of this shit, I'll tell you what I know. James likes to go camping. I think he's hiding in Yosemite. He told me that's where he would go if he was in trouble," Ethan lies, trying to save himself.

"That's the weakest bullshit I have ever heard. I'm closer to shooting you now." The man steps closer to Ethan. His pistol gleams in the low light.

"OK. Yes, that's a lie. James will go stay with his sister. She's in Chicago," Ethan lies again.

"James doesn't have a fucking sister," the man spits.

"Well, then, fuck all of you. Go fuck yourself," Ethan shouts, shivering as he knows what's coming next.

The man calmly raises the pistol to Ethan's forehead and fires.

# CHAPTER 38

# THE ROAD TO SANTA ISABEL

James and Seth drive along a landlocked highway towards Santa Isabel in Puerto Rico. Seth is at the wheel, repeatedly checking the side and center rearview mirrors. James, lost in thought, stares at the landscape.

James thinks about all the anger Seth must feel inside. He thought he was the guy with the worst life, but clearly, Seth has a lot to deal with, too.

"Are you OK? You look kind of nervous," James finally asks.

Seth nods, his eyes still on the mirrors. "I just always watch my back."

In the evening, James and Seth sit in a large upstairs room in a warehouse in Santo Domingo. The sun sets over the ocean, casting a warm glow through the patio door. Two computers rest at opposite ends of a large table, pointed away from each other. Several large boxes block the only door to the room, and the patio has no exit. A new VSAT terminal has been delivered, and Seth has it pointed out the patio door.

James breaks the silence. "So, who is this person who is going to protect us?"

"His name is Tandin Phurba. He is the crown prince of Bhutan," Seth replies casually. "He's going to tell people we are part of his family."

James's eyes widen in disbelief. "How the hell do you know the crown prince of Bhutan?"

Seth smirks. "I tried to scam the Nepalese out of ten million dollars. I had them believing that I could deliver an unknown work of Picasso. Tandin was going to supply part of the money and have a stake in the painting. The truth is that he hates the Nepalese. He figured out that it was a scam, but instead of having me killed, he asked me to do him a favor."

Seth recalls Tandin holding a gun pointed at him. Seth smiles and raises his hands.

"I told them that Tandin was the guy who really had the painting, and I exited the scene. They paid him two million dollars up-front, and he split. It's only his remote location and his security detail that keeps him alive. I became a non-player. He helped me disappear. We are already partners in crime," Seth explains.

Seth continues, his tone turning serious, "The first thing I am going to do is to tell Tandin to withdraw every penny he has in every bank account in the world. I am going to tell him to buy things. It doesn't even matter what. Yachts, paintings, gold bars. I mean anything. When your system hits the world, paper money is going to disappear. Tandin will suddenly be a lot richer compared to everyone else. Once quantum computing is really out there, Bitcoin is going to fail as well. Remember that it is based on encryption, so as soon as encryption is gone, find the biggest whale out there and take his coins. Their value will plunge. We need to convert all of our Bitcoin to gold and goods as soon as we can. I will get Tandin to help us for a cut."

James listens intently as Seth continues, "Your bank heist was scary, but I think most people believe it was conventional. They think it was an inside job. When this thing really hits, it's all over. I hope there aren't too many people around that you care about because a lot of people are going to get hurt badly."

"This is my chance to set some things straight. All the people I hate are the ones who are going to suffer," James says, his voice filled with determination. "Every guy with a million bucks in the bank is suddenly going to be very poor. All the people who saved nothing and have nothing are going to come out of this in pretty good shape, actually. No government is going to be able to handle it. It's too much. I suppose the buyer will be untouched."

"Exactly right. That's the reason they will pay so much. Suddenly, there will be only one group with a viable national reserve. Everyone else is fucked. You better believe that the people we have talked to are already making moves to protect themselves in case they don't win," Seth agrees.

James asks, "What do you think is going to happen?"

Seth stops and thinks, then replies, "I don't know. I just know that the world is going to be turned on its head for about ten years. That's another reason you and I will be safe. We will be in the care of one of the very few people in the world who is still actually rich. Not his government and not any government will be able to get their shit together enough to look at him or come after him. Everyone is going to be trying to just survive."

James looks at Seth with a mix of admiration and fear. "You really thought this through."

"I did. I've just been watching and waiting for you. In twenty years, when the world gets back on its feet, maybe someone will think about looking for us," Seth says thoughtfully.

# CHAPTER 39

# THE WAREHOUSE

"I asked for this exactly. This is an abandoned warehouse. As far as anyone knows, nothing happens here. We are in a new country for the first time in a place no one will think to look. If there is a knock at the door, we have a rope ladder, and we will go out from the patio. We need our next meetings with the Russians, North Koreans, and Chinese. It's time to narrow this down. Tonight, we are meeting the North Koreans again," Seth explains.

"We need to get this done and get out of here, though. Someone delivered a lot of gear, and that is unusual. Word is going to get around, and someone will decide to come check it out. We will stay here tonight, but tomorrow, we leave. We will keep the VSAT with us this time since that is the really weird thing," Seth informs. "If I can avoid having another VSAT terminal delivered, that would be best. Lots of people want laptops."

Seth continues talking, looking straight at James. "So, James, how does it feel to be a genius? You made the most important discovery in human history. You're like Richard Feynman and Albert Einstein. You don't take yourself seriously, but you are going to be known the world over. You have managed to get kicked around, so I guess you never understood your importance. What makes a genius tick? I've talked you into cashing it in, but what really motivates you now?"

James replies, "Well, to some extent, I am just trying to survive at the moment. I have a lifetime of frustration like you. I don't have a problem watching rich people become poor and poor people get rich. I am dispensing some justice. Without you, I would have handed it over to my company and watched someone else get even more rich. The world would have kept marching along as it always does. As you said, I would have been a footnote. You talked me into at least doing something different. The trouble is this is not my world. I am surrounded by danger, and I don't know what I'm doing. My life is in your hands now."

Seth rocks back and stares at the ceiling. He assures James, "This *is* my world. I know what I'm doing. We will get through this, and we will be rich. Your discovery is going to change the world forever. A hundred years from now, people can try to piece it together and decide who won and who lost. Feynman and Einstein didn't get rich and live a great life. Maybe you are smarter than them even."

James shivers. "I'm not exactly looking forward to talking to Samantha. She creeps me out. The backstory has to be terrible. They took whatever she was and made her into something evil. Like you said, she is a performer under penalty of death."

Seth nods. "Everything you say is true, but we need to decide who we are going to deal with. The North Koreans have the money, and they want the secret. That's all we need to know. Just be very careful. They pointed a pretty girl at you for a reason. I don't think you fell for it, but just know in your heart that you will never, ever fuck her."

James laughs nervously. "I got it. I will be careful."

"We're on in ten minutes. I know North Korea steals a lot of Bitcoin. For all I know, they have ten billion in the bank. I have hundreds of accounts they can fill, and I have guys ready to take it and move it. Everyone gets a cut," Seth assures.

James sits still in his chair, inspecting his computer to ensure there are no cameras. Seth puts on a headphone mic and readies his computer. James's computer begins to show activity. His avatar appears at the top corner of the screen, and a window in the center goes from black to showing Samantha. This time, she is wearing even more revealing clothing, her face bathed in a tinge of red light. Her breasts nearly fall out of her top.

"Hello. It's good to see you again. How have you been?" Samantha asks, her voice sultry.

"I'm fine. You seem very relaxed," James responds, trying to maintain his composure.

"What I am is lonely. I don't really get to see anyone. I was looking forward to talking to you," Samantha purrs.

James rolls his eyes. "Well, I don't think we will be going on a date anytime soon."

Samantha's smile doesn't waver. "Anything is possible. Why don't you tell me your name?"

"Well, Samantha, you can pick whatever name you like because it won't be any more real than your name. Why don't we get down to business?" James suggests.

Samantha's tone turns serious. "Life is full of surprises. I like scientists. I would like to know you."

"I think we better just stick to the business at hand. I am not interested in talking about anything else," James insists.

Samantha sighs. "I am disappointed. Fine. We want to meet you to evaluate what you have to offer."

"As I said, we will never meet. Not before and not after our deal. I need money, and then I will hand over the information," James reiterates.

Samantha's eyes narrow. "Then we need to give you half and then evaluate what you give us."

James shakes his head. "If you want it, you need to take a chance. We can hand it over to other people just as fast and just as easily. You need to decide if you want it or not."

"I'm sad that we can't have any sort of trust between us. You look like a nice guy. I wish I could be close to you," Samantha says softly.

James chuckles. "My avatar looks like a nice guy? None of this has anything to do with trust. You want something, and I have it. Our price is fifteen billion delivered by Bitcoin. We can verify the money, and we can deliver the goods."

Samantha's expression hardens. "I want this to go in a different direction. I want to take care of you, and I want you to trust me. We will deliver the money if we get what we want. We have to know that we are getting the real thing."

James's patience wears thin. "I can't be more clear about this. We have demonstrated that we have the technology. I have no intention of meeting you or anyone else."

"I want you to think about it. I am here for you when you want me. Until next time," Samantha says, her tone final.

The screen goes black. James pushes his chair back and looks at Seth, who walks over from across the table.

"That went about how I thought it might. She is a honey trap, about the deadliest kind there is. Once they put you in irons, she might come see you just for kicks. We aren't getting anywhere with these people," Seth states.

James nods. "We can keep them on hold, but I agree. I don't think they will be our buyer. I think they are convinced that they can get away with grabbing the goods and paying nothing."

"OK. Let's call it a night. Tomorrow, we will talk to the Chinese," Seth concludes.

# CHAPTER 40

# ANOTHER DAY, ANOTHER DEAL

The next morning, James and Seth wake up in the same room in the warehouse. They had slept on the ground next to the computers, using only blankets and pillows. James wakes up first and sits on the ground. Seth sits up shortly after.

"Pretty great accommodations, don't you think?" Seth jokes.

James groans. "That kind of sucked. When are we going to eat and shower?"

"There is a hotel in the next town that I want to use. We can pay cash there, too. I'll pay and let you in some back door. I don't want us seen together. That might raise suspicion," Seth explains.

James raises an eyebrow. "What suspicion? It's not like there aren't gay people in Puerto Rico."

Seth laughs. "Sure, but remember, the Russians know our names and what we look like. They are looking for two guys. Two random American white guys wandering around a cheap hotel in Santo Domingo might cause talk. There's no guarantee that anyone knows enough to be dangerous, and as far as I know, nobody knows we are here, but if it's easy to be careful, we should be."

James nods in agreement. “OK. I guess that means we also don’t eat together.”

“I will bring food to the car. We will drive somewhere,” Seth assures. “So, when do we meet the Chinese?” James asks.

“Soon. In thirty minutes,” Seth replies.

“How do you keep arranging all this?” James wonders aloud.

Seth shrugs. “Look, think of that as need to know. Besides, it’s too late for doubts now. The only way out is through.”

James chuckles. “It still amazes me that you were an Alpheus executive.” Seth grins. “Guys like me are all over the place. The higher-ups sometimes just need to get things done, and it takes guys like me to make things happen sometimes. Now I have really found my place in the world. You and I are a team. We can each do things the other person can’t. Without each other, both of us were worth a lot less. I’m looking forward to living out my days with you.”

Seth smiles broadly, then turns serious. “Please get ready for the call.”

James and Seth position themselves in front of their computers. Seth raises his eyebrows at James.

“Be careful with these guys. They didn’t claim to know anything about us, but so far, they have been the most overtly threatening,” Seth warns.

James’s avatar appears at the top corner of his screen, and a black rectangle brightens to show a middle-aged, thin Chinese man.

"My name is Quiang Ming. I am replacing Liu Jianguo. To whom am I speaking?" the man asks.

"You can call me whatever you like. I prefer to stay mysterious. What happened to the guy we talked to before?" James inquires.

"He was assigned other duties. I am taking over this process," Ming explains.

James leans forward. "Well, I can summarize for you where we left things. Liu Jianguo offered five billion, and we need fifteen. We have multiple buyers, so we don't have a lot of patience."

"I think you should realize that most of your buyers simply want to find you and kill you. You would do well to listen to me and do as I say," Ming warns.

James laughs. "Funny, that's what everyone tells us. You need to understand, you will not find out who I am or where I am. I hold the cards. If you want this technology, you have to do things my way."

Ming's tone turns threatening. "Your insubordination is going to get you killed. We are the rightful owners of this technology. We will pay you what is fair for what we receive. You are fortunate that we may offer you money."

James's eyes narrow. "I don't think you understand. You are not exactly coming from a position of strength here. We call the shots. If we don't like what you offer, we move on and get this done. Nobody has a right to anything. The buyer gets the goods."

James is surprised by his newfound confidence and strength.

"You will regret crossing us. If you are wise, you will start working with us now," Ming insists.

James smirks. "And with that, I think it's time to say goodbye. Perhaps you should not have replaced your colleague."

"You are making a terrible mistake," Ming growls.

James hits the big red button, and the screen goes black. He looks up at Seth.

"That was bound to happen with some of these people. The Chinese are used to forcing people to do what they want. I think they took the first guy off the case when he didn't make you do anything either. So, as of this morning, it looks like the North Koreans bombed out and the Chinese bombed out. That leaves the Russians. Fortunately, they have probably been the most serious so far. On the downside, they know a few things about us, so they might be the most dangerous," Seth reflects.

Seth stands up, stretching. "Let's go shower and eat. I'm feeling a little nervous. It's time to move on. This metal box is for the gear. It has a plastic liner. We are going to dump that barrel of acid over the computers and close the lid. I will rent a car with cash. We can dump it in the next town."

James and Seth put the computer equipment in a large,

rectangular container. Seth carefully pours the acid over the equipment, ensuring it stays away from his body. They clear the large boxes away from the door.

"I have made a decision," Seth announces. "We will talk to the Russians tonight. I'm going to take the call. This time it's not a technical sale. It's time to do the deal. I have decided that the Russians are it. I will tell the Russians we will change the deal to ten billion."

James raises an eyebrow. "That sounds like something that perhaps you should have asked me about."

Seth shrugs. "No offense, James, but this is my specialty. You need to trust that I will get us through this and make you happy."

James sighs. "Well, I can't really argue with you. All this weird shit makes very little sense to me. At this point, I just hope I live through it."

Seth glances at James and smiles. "You are going to do more than live through it. You are going to be wildly rich. I'm curious to see what kind of person you turn into with limitless power and fortune."

James chuckles. "I think I'll be the same guy, just drunk and high more often."

"Amen," Seth agrees. "So, tonight, just watch me deal with our Russian friends. I'm dropping the price, so I will add new demands. I'll tell them they need to pay up 100 percent before we transfer. I plan to tell them that we have a complete technical description of the system that we proved and that we will also agree to talk to them as they make it work."

James nods, looking at his small hard drive. "I do have it all recorded and ready. It's hard to believe that my little hard drive is worth ten billion dollars."

The stage is set for the crucial meeting with the Russians. Seth holds his pistol as they cautiously open the door. With no one in sight, they leave the room.

# CHAPTER 41

# BACK AT SEATTLE PD

The same three officers sit around the same plain conference table at the Seattle PD. The first officer is clearly excited.

"We got a break. The guy we were following contacted someone we know who deals in fake passports. We could not read the message, but we know who he is. We cornered and questioned him. He said he just made two passports for guys who sound like Seth and James. He said he was asked if travel to Turkey needed a visa. I think we can assume Seth and James are on their way to Turkey."

The second officer offers, "I can put out a bulletin to watch for two American men entering Istanbul."

"We have their pictures. We can't be sure when they will fly or if they have already flown, but yes, put out the bulletin. We have contacts through Interpol. Tell them these are wanted criminals," replies the first officer.

The third officer just sits and listens. Looking at his watch to see what time it is. He smiles to himself.

As soon as he can, the third officer gathers his things and leaves work. Once again, he drives down a remote road and pulls over. His second phone is taken out of its hiding place.

"They are going to Istanbul. The PD is pretty sure. Their flight will be soon if not already completed," the man says to an unknown recipient.

This time, he doesn't need to return to work. He checks his regular phone map for a nearby restaurant. He will be well paid for this.

# CHAPTER 42

# A PLAN IN MOTION

James and Seth sit in a small farmhouse at the end of a large field in Santa Isabel, Puerto Rico. Their new car is parked outside.

"This is going to be quick," Seth says. "I'll tell the Russians we are ready to deal. Next, you and I are leaving the country. We can backtrack to Mercedita. They have an international airport. I got us fake passports that we are picking up from a safe deposit box in the city. We are flying to Istanbul."

James's expression is tense. "I'm pretty worried about the extent to which you are asking people to do stuff for us. Any connection to anyone makes us vulnerable, and it seems that your associates are not exactly trustworthy. How many people know where we are right now?"

"Probably three. I switch up who I'm working with. I pay people off and say goodbye," Seth replies. "I will pay a kid to go inside and get our passports with a promise of triple the money when he hands them over. We will not go in ourselves."

James's concern deepens. "If you know and trust these people, others can find out that you know them. They are not hiding. We are one step away from the bad guys."

Seth nods. "That's why we are leaving the country. Fake passports have fake names. Once we are in Istanbul, we disappear. I'm not setting up any more computers or SATCOM there. Tonight should be our last meeting. We can leave right afterwards."

James takes a deep breath. "I think there's a chance one or some of your people can be compromised. I would be happier to be on the road than here."

"OK. Let's set up," Seth agrees.

James and Seth set up their computer gear on an old wooden table. "How do we know that our comms don't give us away?" James asks.

"I explained this before. Don't worry. I hire a new team every time. It works as I showed you. Satellite terminal to VPN on a virtual machine to foreign connection. All the equipment gets trashed. We will be long gone before anyone can track us down," Seth reassures.

James's worry persists. "What I'm worried about is someone who knows where we are going getting grabbed. We will transit two international airports. If anyone knows where we are coming from or where we are going, they got us."

"It's true that a flight is not as safe as a boat, but we need to put some serious distance between today and tomorrow. You can take it easy. I got this one," Seth says confidently.

Seth switches on a laptop. An avatar appears in the top corner of the screen. The meeting proceeds with the Russians. Seth explains the lowered price and gives Bitcoin instructions. The Russian agrees.

# CHAPTER 43

# MOVING ON

"The drive to the airport is only twenty-four minutes," Seth reports. "We will stay in a hotel tonight, and I will get the passports in the morning. We are buying the tickets in person with cash. That is acceptable here."

"Seth, for the record, my life is now in your hands. I have no control over anything," James says, his face taut with tension.

"You keep saying that. Just relax. I've got this. As I said, we are done with computer meetings," Seth explains. "We are about to ditch the VSAT terminal and computer equipment. When I find a good spot to pull over, we will look for a dumping place somewhere. If it is found two weeks from now, we don't care."

Seth and James set off in the car. As expected, the drive is short. They stop briefly to dump the gear. In Mercedita, they find a small hotel at the edge of town. Following the usual routine, Seth pays extra cash and gets a remote room.

The next morning, Seth wakes up James. James showers while Seth gets food from the hotel restaurant and brings it to the room.

They drive downtown, and James waits in the car as he watches

Seth approach a kid selling trinkets on the street. The kid goes into the post office and comes out with an envelope. Seth meets the kid a block away and hands him a small pile of cash. Seth comes back to the car with a smile on his face.

At the airport, Seth pays for long-term parking and parks the car, with no intention of ever retrieving it. James inspects his fake passport.

"We need to remember our fake names," says James.

"Write it on your hand, just in case. Just keep it out of sight if they ask you anything. Your birthday, too," Seth instructs. "I will give you plenty of cash. This isn't the US. Cash works here. You want the flight to Istanbul that lands at 4 PM. If they ask you anything, keep your hand below the counter and read it. You are going to a science meeting. If they ask, you have one of those folding travel suits in your bag. You are an experienced traveler."

James has to try very hard to not have a Tourette attack. The interaction with the inspector is actually easier than he expected. He finishes first and sees Seth waving a hand as his inspector. He, too, passes.

"What happened there?" James asks.

"The inspector didn't think I looked like I was going to a science conference, so I spouted off some technical stuff and acted angry. Once we take off, we are really safe," Seth assures.

# CHAPTER 44

# THE FINAL STRETCH

Seth negotiates a room on a high floor at the CVK Park Bosporus Hotel, Istanbul. Istanbul is not such a remote place, so he has to operate similarly to how he would in the US. He still uses cash and his new fake passport. James waits in a corner of the lobby, drinking coffee and trying not to look out of place. James and Seth agreed to separately take elevators to the third floor and meet there to go to the room.

Once inside, Seth explains, "All we are doing now is watching for Bitcoin to show up. I have one last team in the US waiting for our transmission. This time, we will just use an internet café to transmit the contents of your hard drive to the US. They will send it on to Russia. We don't need any special equipment or procedures here. This is the final stretch. The team in the US has a password to access a VPN in Russia. I think that's funny because pretty soon all passwords will be broken."

James asks, "So we have nothing to do? No one to talk to? It's been nonstop for so long. You're telling me that we are just waiting for money now?"

Seth smiles and nods. "Exactly. We're done. We did it. We just need to stay cool and lay low. Tomorrow, we can go out and look around. This is a beautiful city. I'll order room service. I know about Turkish food. Let me order for you."

James reclines on the bed and lets out a big sigh of relief. This nightmare might almost be over.

The next morning, Seth advises James how to carefully exit the hotel. This is a much more metropolitan place, and there will be more people around. There are many international visitors, and it will not be easy to spot a tail.

Seth explains, "James, we are going to take separate elevators to the lobby. I want you to look for a woman and follow her out. Don't talk to her or get her attention. Walk behind her closely enough that it looks like you are together. The last thing we want is to be spotted together as two men. That's what people will be looking for. Keep an eye out for anyone who looks like they are watching you. Exit the lobby and go to the car. I will meet you there. If we get separated, or if you spot a tail, find a way to get to the Hagia Sophia Grand Mosque and go to the ticket counter. I will meet you there exactly at noon. If anything happens, repeat that, and meet me the next day. Here's cash. You can use this to find a place to stay and get around. Hopefully, we just meet at the car and go for a drive. This is almost over, but we still need to be careful. Once we get our Bitcoin, we are going to Bhutan. Then we're free."

# Chapter 45

# Ambushed In Istanbul

Along the bustling streets near the Grand Bazaar Market in Istanbul, Seth is driving James in a rented sports car. Seth is looking and feeling confident. "James, we made our sales pitch, we found a customer, and we have an agreement," Seth boasts. "Now we wait a day, and I ask my guys to check Bitcoin. This is almost over."

"I have to hand it to you. I feel like we went through a lot of dangerous stuff, but we are here. We are in a foreign country under fake IDs. I do think we are probably safe now," James replies.

As they drive between two tall buildings, two cars speed up from the front and one from behind, blocking their path. They are trapped in a funnel between the tall buildings.

Two men with rifles appear on third-floor balconies, and three men get out of each car. Seth slams the car into reverse, hitting the car behind them, running over one of the men, and pushing the nose of the car out of the way. The men on the third floor open fire, but Seth speeds away.

The two cars that were in front of them give chase. Seth, demonstrating impressive evasive driving skills, drives the wrong way down a two-lane road, swerving between oncoming cars, honking the horn, and flashing headlights. The chase continues until Seth clips an oncoming car and loses control. Their car crashes into a barrier, injuring both Seth and James.

Men from the pursuing cars pull them out of the wreckage. Black cloth bags are pulled over their heads, their hands are cable-tied behind their backs, and they are put into two separate cars. Two men guard each captive while one drives.

# CHAPTER 46

# CAPTURED

James wakes up in a dark room, bound to a large chair. A table and another chair sit in front of him. A door opens, flooding the room with bright light, blinding him.

In another room, Seth wakes up, similarly bound.

"You are Seth Lawrence. What is your role in this transaction?" an interrogator asks Seth.

Seth smiles defiantly. "Nice to meet you. I'm not telling you anything."

Seth thinks of Adira and what could have been. He knows what's coming next.

The two interrogators exchange glances. One nods, and the other takes out a pistol, shooting Seth in the forehead.

James, still bound in the first room, hears a shot, the door close, and footsteps approach. An interrogator sits in front of him, turning on a spotlight.

"You are James Cathcart," the interrogator states.

James, trying to remain calm, responds, "I'm not telling you anything." "That's funny. That's what the dead guy said," the interrogator retorts before injecting James in the leg. Terrified, James pulls at his restraints. Within seconds, he passes out. As his consciousness fades, James thinks of Seth. He is angry for Seth bringing them to this end, but Seth was his only real friend in the world. Now his friend is dead.

James wakes up in pitch blackness, unable to determine the size or layout of the room. He can feel that some of his clothes have been removed. His hands and feet remain bound to a chair. The room is very cold. James is terrified.

Faint screams grow louder, turning into the unmistākable sounds of a person in agony. Mechanical noises accompany the tortured screams. James struggles against his restraints but cannot escape. Sounds come from another part of the room in front of him. More agony. He hears motorized sounds. A person is being tortured.

After a time, the door behind him opens. It is still too dark to see. A bag is placed over his head, and his chair is wheeled away. The bag is removed, and a bright light shines on his face. Instruments of torture are laid out on a table in front of him.

"James, what you heard were others we have broken. This will be your fate," the interrogator says.

James, now desperate, asks, "What do you want?"

"I want to know everything about your quantum computing system.

Everything," the interrogator demands.

"What's to stop you from killing me anyway?" James challenges.

The interrogator leans in. "Well, you don't have much of a choice. You can trust me or die screaming. I know how to use all of these instruments. We will get from you whatever we want."

James, seeing no other option, offers, "OK. I will tell you if you let me go."

"Well, let's get started. Tell me how to do it," the interrogator presses.

James tries to buy time. "The only way this will ever work is if you set me up to do it and I do it for you."

"Well, we could go back to hurting you," the interrogator threatens.

James remains defiant. "Threaten all you want. Without my direct assistance, you have nothing, and you will fail."

The interrogator considers this for a moment. "I will ask about your request. Meanwhile, good night."

The interrogator injects James again, causing him to shout before passing out.

The interrogator mutters to himself, "Let's get out of this fucking place. I want to go home."

# CHAPTER 47

# BUILDING THE QUANTUM COMPUTER

James is drugged and transported deep inside Russia. He wakes up bathed in clean clothes in a white room. Bright sunlight comes through a tall window. He makes his way to the door, but it is locked. "James, you are in the Kavka Lab. When you are ready, a team wants your instructions about what to build," says a disembodied voice from a speaker in the room. "Your door opens in ten minutes."

James is strangely relaxed. He's alive, but his best and only friend is dead. He immediately hatches a plan. He will not give these people the secret. The system is very complicated. He can drag this out for months. He knows how difficult all the necessary equipment is to find.

Later, James meets a small crew and describes the equipment he requires. He is living a luxurious prison life. He eats tasty meals and sleeps soundly.

Weeks later, the Russians have constructed a lab under James's direction.

Natalia, a Russian quantum computing expert, approaches James.

"James, my name is Natalia. I have been brought to help you build a quantum computer," she introduces herself.

James looks at Natalia. She is beautiful. He can't believe that his forced companion is so attractive.

James, wary and tired, responds, "You are helping a prisoner. How do you feel about that?"

Natalia's expression is resolute. "I have been working on this my whole life. I don't really care about politics or money. I just want to succeed."

James nods, finding a kindred spirit. "Well, at least that is noble. I have to help you, or they will kill me."

"I know you have made this work before. I will help you make it work again," Natalia reassures.

Again, James is amazed. She is beautiful and smart. She is so near and yet so far.

"Well, if you are an expert, you already know a lot about what we need to do. We will use hydrogen atoms since they have one electron. That electron is our qubit. We need a cryo system to cool the atoms. We must trap a single atom and measure its quantum state without disturbing it. Only atomic interactions are allowed to change quantum states. We also need to change the state when we wish. As you know, quantum states are our qubits. As you also know, heat destroys quantum states. Quantum computers need to be kept very cold," James explains.

"We already have a liquid helium system ready for you," Natalia informs.

James continues, "I will need to build a millimeter wave transmitter. It operates at 100 GHz. That is what I use to measure the quantum state. The probe photon energy is low enough that it can react to the spin state without changing it."

Natalia nods. "I had ideas along that line, but I never tried them. We tried everything that has failed already."

"Show me to the lab then. Let's get started," James says, feigning cooperation.

Men and women are working in the lab. Weeks pass.

James's only joy is his interactions with Natalia. Even at a distance, he admires her. He sees her every day. Every time he does, he fantasizes about the life he might have had with her. The way she looks at him, he knows she is thinking about him, too. If they were not forced to be captor and slave, things could have been so different. As the weeks pass, James grows to love Natalia.

"What is your progress?" Natalia asks. "You are a good worker. I admire your persistence."

"I am making slow progress. This really is torture," James admits.

Natalia looks at him with sympathy. "James, I know you wish you could be doing this for good reasons. I know you are a good man. I wish we could have worked together in another world."

James smiles sadly. "Natalia, I also wish we could have met in normal life. You are everything I ever wanted to find in a woman. You are beautiful and brilliant."

Natalia hands James a small statue of the Virgin Mary. "James, this is a religious relic that has been passed down my family. I want you to have it."

James is overwhelmed. "Natalia, I am touched. Thank you so much. You and I are stuck in this madness, but in another place, we could learn about each other. I wish I could know you."

Natalia smiles and puts her hand on James's shoulder. She turns and walks away, and James hides his face so no one can see the tears in his eyes. The irony is overwhelming. James stands next to a woman he loves, but she is his captor. They respect each other's work, but they are enemies. James feels like this is a fitting conclusion to his miserable life. The one person who cared about him is dead.

James finally makes a plan. He feels like his life has become a sad movie. Despite whatever happened, James is at heart an honest man. Seth obviously led him astray, and now he is paying the price. His fate is sealed. He can't possibly let the Russians have quantum computing. He would single-handedly ruin the world. He should have seen this coming months ago. Even if he could miraculously survive this situation, the world he would face would have been a disaster.

James contacts Natalia via a laptop screen. "Natalia, your chiller is not getting cold enough for the system to work. I need to look at it and figure out what is going wrong. I need some time alone. Please have your people stay out of my lab for at least a day. Your people can interrogate me and threaten me again tomorrow."

Natalia agrees. "Fine. I will tell our people to give you a day alone." James is alone in the laboratory. He shuts his laptop and stands up, reaching for a two-foot metal cylinder that controls the lab's overhead crane. James looks up at a camera and gives the middle finger. Natalia and several soldiers rush to the door of the laboratory.

# CHAPTER 48

# THE ENDGAME

James sits on the laboratory platform, holding the small statue in his hand that Natalia gave him. A tear streams from one eye as his face winces and twitches. His chest moves rapidly as he stops consuming oxygen. The statuette of Mary falls from his hand.

The Russians finally open the lab doors thirty minutes later, but James is dead. With the lab doors open, the helium has cleared out of the room. Two men in white coats and one soldier in green stand with Natalia next to James's slumped form.

Natalia, looking at the equipment, says, "I have looked at the quantum state maintenance. It is not working at all. I think James tricked us. All he had to do was tell us one wrong thing, and it will never work. If he were still alive, we could get it from him, but he's dead now. He managed to give himself a painless death. He just went to sleep. He lied about the millimeter wave photons not destroying the quantum state. I don't know if it's just the frequency, or if he was doing something special with polarization. All I know is that beaming an atom with 100 GHz photons kills the state immediately. It is useless. We have no solution, and we have a dead scientist."

# CHAPTER 49

# PICKING UP THE PIECES

Back at Alpheus headquarters in Seattle, several executives stand in James Cathcart's former lab. One man, Joel Franken, leafs through a notebook on a laboratory table.

"Frank, James didn't leave behind much, but we did find one notebook in his office. I think he missed it when he left," Joel says.

Frank Hanson looks curious. "Does it tell you anything?"

Joel nods. "He wrote down that maintaining the quantum state required interrogation with swept frequency terahertz."

Frank frowns. "He never let anyone really see what he was doing. We can look at all the equipment that he purchased."

"There could be some difficult details. We need to find another expert in the field. I can't do this stuff. If you read his resume and look at his experience, I am sure we can find someone sort of equivalent," Joel suggests.

Frank looks thoughtful. "Use of terahertz is a pretty general idea. Is there enough there to make it work?"

Joel points to the notebook. "James wrote that resonance can be interrogated with broadband terahertz to determine electron spin state. This is stuff I know nobody else is trying. Everyone else is using lasers. Single photon energy is so high that one photon can change a quantum state. This is really different."

Frank's expression turns serious. "If this gets into the wrong hands, it will not be launched in a controlled way. We wanted to take it step by step, make money, but keep the world rolling. We already saw panic ensue from the Bank of England heist. If quantum computing emerges, no bank is safe, so no money is safe. There will be chaos."

Joel agrees. "I think it's more likely that some government is going to want to hack military secrets and diplomatic communication. They might slow roll it."

Frank nods. "It depends on who it is. If it's China, I agree. If it's North Korea, I think they will grab as much money as they can, and they will not care much about how much chaos they produce."

# CHAPTER 50

# DARK FUTURE

In the Alpheus headquarters laboratory, two scientists stand in front of a bank of equipment and computer monitors. The equipment is very active, with many lights blinking and traces on oscilloscopes.

Joel turns to Frank. "What are we going to do with this if we really make it work?"

Frank smiles. "Well, we're not going to rob banks. Our government will pay handsomely to decrypt everyone else. My guess is that they are going to keep it secret as long as they can. The longer they can read everything, the more they benefit."

Joel looks skeptical. "So how does it make us rich?"

Frank explains, "We are going to change computing fundamentally. Computer simulation has always suffered from slow computers. We spend so much making the biggest, fastest computers we can. If Alpheus can sell you a computer that is thousand times faster, you will pay thousand times more."

"But if we sell quantum computers, anyone can break encryption. Then the world collapses. You can't be sure that we will still make any money in that situation. Who is going to have the money to pay us?" Joel argues.

Frank shakes his head. "James and Seth probably tried to sell it for money and didn't care what happened. We need the world to keep working. Alpheus will also sell new encryption. We will make a ton of money there, too. Quantum computing used to crack encryption is beaten by new forms of encryption. A stream of single photons can pass keys. Any interference is detectable. There are ways to get around the problem."

Joel looks relieved. "That sounds good, but there's going to certainly be a period of upheaval."

Frank nods. "We will let the USG have it for a while so they can take everything. Then we release it to the world after we patch it."

Joel sighs. "That sounds like a corporate board speech, and I don't think it's going to work so well. I think world markets are going to tank and Alpheus might find itself without much money. If we figure it out, maybe we should use it to get money."

Frank frowns. "I don't think you will talk the board into stealing."

Joel looks contemplative. "I just want you to think about what is really going to happen. Maybe Seth and James had the right idea, even though it probably killed them."

Frank looks down, conflicted. "James wanted to change the world. This could have gone well. Seth took him down a bad path, and now they are both probably dead. This is still going to happen. We just need to be smart and try to not destroy the world in the process."

Intense work is being done in a bustling lab to understand and harness the power of quantum computing, hinting at the uncertain but inevitable impact it will have on the world. Quantum computing offers opportunities for great good and great evil. Either way, it offers immense wealth, so Alpheus will keep going.

Problems that would take years or decades to solve can be completed in seconds. In 1981, Richard Feynman said, "Nature isn't classical, dammit, and if you want to make a simulation of nature, you'd better make it quantum mechanical, and by golly it's a wonderful problem, because it doesn't look so easy."

www.ingramcontent.com/pod-product-compliance
Lightning Source LLC
LaVergne TN
LVHW022051200926
848481LV00003B/866
* 9 7 9 8 3 4 9 2 2 9 6 8 8 *